Praise for *Battle Ready*

"The best time to be strengthened against the enemy's tactics of doubt, disappointment, and devastation is before he makes his first move toward us. We all desperately need the biblical guidance and preparation found in *Battle Ready*!"

Lysa TerKeurst, *New York Times* bestselling author and president of Proverbs 31 Ministries

"The most difficult fights we will face in this life will not be on the outside; they will be within our own hearts and minds. As someone who has struggled with depression and anxiety throughout my life, I know this firsthand. *Battle Ready* will help encourage, empower, and equip you to live in true victory."

Holley Gerth, bestselling author of *Fiercehearted*

"Do you ever wonder why you struggle at times with doubt and insecurity, even though you are a follower of Christ? When trials and troubles come your way, does your faith seem to falter rather than flourish? *Battle Ready* will equip and empower you, teaching you where to park your mind during such difficult times. Its practical advice and pen-to-paper reflection sections, coupled with the truths of Scripture sprinkled throughout, will enable you to avoid defeat and discouragement and walk confidently in faith instead. Highly recommended."

Karen Ehman, national speaker, *New York Times* bestselling author of *Keep It Shut* and *Listen, Love, Repeat*, wife, and mother of three

"*Battle Ready* is a field manual for the mind. If you desire to think more like Christ, its truths, stories, personal applications, and discoveries will undoubtedly lead you to renewed places of peace, hope, and life."

Elisa Morgan, speaker and author of *The Beauty of Broken*

Praise for *Rest Now*

"If you are ready to be set free from the nagging stress of feeling chronically overwhelmed, then *Rest Now* is the book you have been looking for. Filled with practical takeaways and transformational ideas, it is sure to gain a place at the top of your favorite books list."

Mandy Arioto, president and CEO of MOPS International

"We all need a friend who understands the struggles of life. More importantly, we need a friend who points us to Jesus. Kelly Balarie does both in *Rest Now*. With transparent and tender compassion, Kelly shows us how to access the peace of God—as well as His joy—even in the midst of chaos."

Joanna Weaver, author of *Having a Mary Heart in a Martha World*

"I jumped at the chance to read *Rest Now*—not just because Kelly Balarie is known for her positive encouragement but because *I am so tired*. God's true rest eludes me. If I'm being honest, I am so far from living in that place that I don't even know how to aspire to it. *Rest Now* is full of practical advice for identifying the lies we tell ourselves that keep us from being able to embrace rest, as well as straightforward tips for overcoming the barriers we've put in the way of getting there—and ways to implement boundaries so we can remain there. This book shows us we can have that beautiful, peaceful life of rest God promised. Not someday. Not later. *Now*."

Kelly O'Dell Stanley, author of *Praying Upside Down*, *Designed to Pray*, and *InstaPrayer: Prayers to Share*

"In *Rest Now*, Kelly Balarie provides a real-life and applicable antidote for all who find themselves shuffling for approval in the pursuit of *more*, *busy*, and *perfection*: the ability and the wisdom to rest in the here and now, knowing we were made for this life by a God who simply wants us to *rest in His arms* when we feel weary."

Kara Lawler, author of *Everywhere Holy*

TAKE
EVERY
THOUGHT
CAPTIVE

TAKE
EVERY
THOUGHT
CAPTIVE

EXCHANGE LIES OF THE ENEMY
FOR THE MIND OF CHRIST

KELLY BALARIE

BakerBooks
a division of Baker Publishing Group
Grand Rapids, Michigan

© 2023 by Kelly Balarie

Published by Baker Books
a division of Baker Publishing Group
PO Box 6287, Grand Rapids, MI 49516-6287
www.bakerbooks.com

Printed in the United States of America

Library of Congress Cataloging-in-Publication Data
Names: Balarie, Kelly, 1978– author.
Title: Take every thought captive : exchange lies of the enemy for the mind of Christ / Kelly Balarie.
Description: Grand Rapids, MI : Baker Books, a division of Baker Publishing Group, [2023] | Includes bibliographical references.
Identifiers: LCCN 2022035883 | ISBN 9780801094989 (paperback) | ISBN 9781540902993 (casebound) | ISBN 9781493439492 (ebook)
Subjects: LCSH: Thought and thinking—Religious aspects—Christianity.
Classification: LCC BV4598.4 .B35 2023 | DDC 230—dc23/eng/20220930
LC record available at https://lccn.loc.gov/2022035883

23 24 25 26 27 28 29   7 6 5 4 3 2 1

To the biggest-little joys of my life, the ones who make me smile bigger than anything, the two highly effective teachers at shaping me into the image of Jesus: Michael and Madison.

I love you more than you know, more than words, and more than I probably ever let on. I am proud of you. Madison, you are the most courageous girl around! You overcome time and time again. Michael, you are a boy after God's own heart. This book, and all that is contained herein, is for you.

Undoubtedly, God has great plans for you, and I know, 100 percent, that God will see them through!

Contents

Introduction: The Call to Seize the Mind of Christ 11

PART 1 Arm Up for Battle

1. Become a Blank Slate 19
2. Be a Warrior! 29
3. Believe You're Worthy of a Changed Mind 41

PART 2 Be Strong of Heart, Be Strong of Mind

4. Develop a Heart of Gold 59
5. Allow Experience to Transcend Knowledge 69
6. Respond, Don't React 81
7. Say, "Shut Up, Devil!" 91
8. Avoid This Mentality at All Costs 101
9. Adopt These Eight Heart Postures 113

PART 3 Start Now: Take Every Thought Captive

10. The Stop/Start Process 131
11. Break Down the Lie of "I Am Not Enough or Don't Have Enough" 149

12. Break Down the Lie of "I Shoulda, Woulda, or Coulda" 159
13. Break Down the Lie of "I'm Not Wanted, I'm Lonely and Rejected" 167
14. Break Down the Lie of "I Can't Really Trust God" 177
15. Break Down the Lie of "I Have to Do Something about This" 191
16. An Overcomer's Guide to Keeping Thoughts Captive 205

Conclusion: What You Need to Know to Carry On 229
Acknowledgments 235
Appendix: Tools for Sustaining Victory 237
Notes 245

Introduction

The Call to Seize the Mind of Christ

God's thoughts belong to the world of spirit, man's to the world
of the intellect, and while spirit can embrace intellect, the human
intellect can never comprehend spirit.

A. W. Tozer, An Anthology

Only truth sets free. So, I'll start with truth: I write to help
me. Every book I've written started from the fact that I
need help from God. In this, God has always shown up
for me. It's a biblical principle: those who seek, find.

First I wrote *Fear Fighting*, and He released not only me from
fear but countless others. Then I wrote about being *Battle Ready*,
and I—along with a host of other believers—became armed to
overcome. Later, when I was out of steam from hard work, *Rest
Now* gave me and my fellow colaborers deeper connection and
union with God. Now, this book, *Take Every Thought Captive*,
will be a release of all the worries, burdens, and lies kept deep
within our minds. In this we will stop only surviving and start

thriving. We will start thinking, walking, and loving like Christ. We will gain His mind and stop living by ours.

The shift will be cataclysmic.

Take Every Thought Captive aims to be a practical, return-to resource—a mark-it-up, underline, and write-in-the-margin book. By taking every thought captive, you will be able to live out God's purposes and intents for your life. This book will be a mental arsenal to see you through a life that is honoring to God.

New friend, I've learned that when the going gets tough, a tough mind *has to* get going by taking every thought captive. Much of the material herein is time-tested and hard-learned through hard-fought trials. What is contained in this book is *His* action plan, His wisdom, and His truth. I've gleaned it through trials like an eating disorder, financial trouble, health issues, family distress, uncertainty, relationship conflicts, and insecurity.

I release His Word and how to apply it with great hope it will change your life just like mine.

As a result of the learning God has walked me through, I don't have as much down-in-the-gutter thinking. Now, on those days when lies tell me that I'm a horrible mom, when I think everyone is against me, when someone criticizes me or downright rejects me, I have a go-to plan. I more quickly move from mind-yuck to God's light.

There is no sinking sand when you stand with Jesus's thoughts in you.

Absolutely one of the most powerful things a person can do is to let Jesus's thoughts become their thoughts. The mind of Christ is radically assuring. It whispers things like, *The storm is conquerable, through Me.*

In this, rather than believing God's Word cerebrally, truth is owned wholeheartedly and entirely. Doubt goes and faith comes. Hopelessness vanishes and hope comes.

Taking every thought captive is the avenue by which the mind of Christ fills our minds. It is where His thoughts become ours. It is where we don't strive for faith but walk by His faith.

You should know I am focused and targeted with my words in this book. My goal is to set people free.

I've found God moves when I hit with strength. When I speak plainly. My hope is that doing so will shave hard times, years, tears, and trauma off your journey in radical ways. Then you will become like Christ, thinking as He thinks, acting as He acts, and loving like He loves, more quickly. This is 100 percent not *my* work, the work of Kelly Balarie. It is the Lord's work, which is why the Word of God is so front and center, active, and prominent in this book. It will save you from the world, from your own mind, from your fears, from your marriage difficulties, from the thought that you are not enough, from stress, from anxiety, and from pressures megaphoning in your life. Jesus saves. And He will save you, because that is His business. He is better than any human at setting people free. You don't have to shape up to receive from Him. He died for sinners. So go ahead and trash the self-berating and self-condemning, bullying thoughts that demand you *Do better! Shape up! Get it together!*

The pressure and burdens don't belong to you anymore. Let Jesus help you. He is good at carrying hard loads.

With Jesus, we will find release from thoughts like:

I'm not enough.

I can't.

I won't ever . . .

I make terrible decisions.

I'm a loser.

I'm crazy.

I'm impossible.

There is no way that . . .

I've made a horrible mistake by . . .

God is angry at me.

I don't belong.

I'm lonely.

I'm not enough.

I'm fat and ugly.

I'm a burden.

Something is wrong with me.

I have to please people to be liked.

I'm stupid.

I'm ashamed.

I'm useless.

No matter the unruly feeling pestering you underneath these thoughts, the truth remains: "we are more than conquerors through him who loved us" (Rom. 8:37) and "[we] can do all things through Him who strengthens [us]" (Phil. 4:13 NASB). We can rest on the fact that all the grace we need, we have because of Jesus!

When we feel that changing our minds is too impossible, which I have felt on many a day, it is wise to remember there is no war that is unwinnable with the Captain of the Lord's army. The Lord of Hosts is on our side! It doesn't matter how scared we may feel about the advancing armies. If we feel the size of ants and we see giants. None of it matters! Available to us is not old mindsets but rather a better mind: the mind of Christ.

Dear one, this is 100 percent accessible to you, because, as you will see, the mind of Christ is available to you in God's Word. And the result of His mind will be awe-inspiring to those you want to reach for Christ.

They may even ask you, "How is it that you have so much joy and peace when so much fear and turmoil are surrounding us? How are you okay with all this going on in our world?" They won't see doubt or fear on your face; they'll see your faith in an unshakable God.

And you will also have the humility to know that it's not at all your work but *God's*.

The mind of Christ can change everything, if you let it. Never doubt the supernatural arming power of an armed-up God. He, Himself, in all His glory, might, strength, and power—working from the inside out of you—is enough to take any beast, wall, or stronghold down. Take courage! The size of your God far outweighs any issues in your mind.

DECLARATION

I have the mind of Christ.

Homework

Identify the bully thoughts that berate, condemn, or torment you. Write them down. Call them out.

Note for the Reader

This is my prayer for you: *Father, I thank You for every reader of this book. I ask You to supernaturally meet them in every way their soul, mind, heart, and spirit needs. I ask Your Holy Spirit to move in powerful and profound ways. I thank You for the personal testimonies You've had me share. I pray that my breakthrough will become theirs. I know Your faithfulness is going to move. The strength of Your Word will go forth and do what You've sent it to do. Thank You for Your faithfulness. Bless each reader deeply and profoundly. In Jesus's name. Amen.*

Prayer

Father, we want to release the lies of the enemy to gain the mind of Christ. We want to think like You, talk like You, and walk like You. We want to look like You and portray You to everyone we meet. I pray that when people look at us, they don't see us but rather see Jesus. May they see Your love, Your grace, Your compassion, Your hope, Your life, and Your truth shining out. I pray we don't get in Your way. I pray for You to come and do the work in us,

Holy Spirit, with power and quickness. Release us from mental prisons, from self-doubt, from fear. Renew us with Your truth, Your ways, and Your hope. Strengthen our inner selves as we read this book. Show us the paths of life and the ways everlasting. In Jesus's all-saving, ever-working name. Amen.

Free Download

Assess your mental strength. Take the "Take Every Thought Captive Assessment" to discover your areas for growth. Visit www.itakethoughtscaptive .com to download.

PART 1

Arm Up
for Battle

1

Become a Blank Slate

I have since learned that the most mature believer is the one who is bent over, leaning most heavily on the Lord, and admitting his total inability to do anything without Christ. The greatest Christian is not the one who has achieved the most but rather the one who has received the most.

Jim Cymbala, *Fresh Faith*

I love being used by God to lead people to water. Thirsty people with impossible problems experience radical change. God feeds the hungry and gives drink to the thirsty. This is why, no matter how uncomfortable it may be, I try to live my life in want of Jesus. I want Him to squeeze me like a lemon, so He gets every bit of juice from my life.

But the opposite of this sort of posture is what creates issues. Let's begin with a story that will better explain what I mean.

Two ladies requested mentorship with me. Both seemed equally eager. Their education level was on par, they shared common hopes for the future, they were approximately the same age, and both had big dreams. They also both had apparent needs. But, as I met in private with each of them, I couldn't help but notice the two were radically different.

One came as a blank slate, with an open heart and mind and a hungry sense to encounter God. She said, "I want to know all God has to tell me or show me." I think she knew, underneath, that she needed help. The stakes were high. She was hungry.

The other came knowing a whole lot about God. In our first meeting, she said, "I just want to talk." She wanted me to be a sounding board for her mind-rehash and regurgitations. She wanted to voice her worries and stresses. It appeared she was content staying in the pit she was in—as long as she could talk about it, which she did 99 percent of the time. I couldn't get a word in edgewise.

I knew within minutes person number two wasn't going to experience life-change. She was hardly an open slate; she was a closed door.

Jesus asked the lame man, "Do you want to be healed?" (John 5:6 ESV). Many of us should confront that same question today: Do we want to be healed?

I assume you do, or you wouldn't be reading this, but if you don't, you may as well shut the book. It will waste space in your life. Its material will gain cobwebs in your mind, and you may as well be watching TV.

Only blank-slated minds get new story lines crafted by the Master Author Himself. If you insist on your own story and opinions, the "Author and Perfecter of faith" (Heb. 12:2 AMP) may as well write His story somewhere else.

Ever noticed? God doesn't force Himself on people who don't want Him.

What We Risk

God's thoughts are not our thoughts. We cannot come opinionated, full of our own thinking—our rights, our formula, our way, our plan of what should happen—and name it God's. Pride has a hard time seeing itself. Pride can't see its own rear end. Many of us figure our thinking is right thinking.

As my friend and author Joanna Weaver once said to me, we can be right and still be wrong. We may even have truth. But without love to accompany it, is that truth right? We must have God's thinking so that even our best thinking doesn't become tainted with self-righteousness, self-promotion, or self-pity.

God's thoughts are not ours. "'For my thoughts are not your thoughts, neither are your ways my ways,' declares the LORD" (Isa. 55:8).

What if our whole breakthrough is less about what we think and more about what God thinks? What if He cares less about our rights and more about His glory, His thoughts, and His intentions working through us?

The most self-absorbed people constantly think about themselves. We don't want to be absorbed in our thoughts; we want to be absorbed in His thoughts.

For a long time, I thought, *I should do this. I will do that. They should know this. I think this. I am right. I am going here. I am doing this. I need to say that. They have to hear this. I have to defend myself.* My mind was a loose cannon, shooting in every direction. I didn't think God cared about my rapid-fire responses, unhinged mouth, emotionally motivated responses, opinionated determinations, or assumptions. I didn't think much about how things pleased Him—I thought about me. What made me feel good. What I wanted. How I wanted people to treat me.

Do you find yourself thinking this way too? Do your hurts, opinions, summations, and categorizations fill your mind?

I'm learning that relying on me often causes me to rebel against Him. But, more importantly, this is how God sees this sort of thinking:

Stop deceiving yourselves. If you think you are wise by this world's standards, you need to become a fool to be truly wise. For the wisdom of this world is foolishness to God. As the Scriptures say,

> "He traps the wise
> in the snare of their own cleverness."
> (1 Cor. 3:18–19 NLT)

The Lord knows the thoughts and reasonings of the [humanly] wise and recognizes how futile they are. (v. 20 AMPC)

For if any person thinks himself to be somebody [too important to condescend to shoulder another's load] when he is nobody [of superiority except in his own estimation], he deceives and deludes and cheats himself. (Gal. 6:3 AMPC)

When we think thoughts of self, we cheat ourselves. When we think we are wise, we are actually fools. For instance, when I "think myself" too good, too above some task, too set in my ways, too fearful of service, too embarrassed to submit to God, too put-out to love, I cheat myself of the goodness gleaned in enduring awkwardness. I miss God's treasure. "God opposes the proud but shows favor to the humble" (James 4:6).

Opposing God's way for our own way is foolish. "*A fool* does not delight in understanding, but in revealing *his own mind*" (Prov. 18:2 NASB). Fools have all the right answers and independent spirits that rely on their own ways. But the bottom line is: "The thought of foolishness is sin" (24:9 KJV).

Fools set on revealing their own minds are not open to the mind of Christ; they are not in the right position to be blank slates. They are in sin. They know it all. They are set in their own way. They are blind to pride. They are determined that God should do things their way. Rather than seeing God's goodness, they get opposed due to their pride and, as a result, they become angry, bitter, and resentful.

The Practicalities of Coming as a Blank Slate

What does a blank slate look like? Who, in the Bible, was a blank slate?

Jesus.

He said, "Very truly I tell you, the Son can do nothing by himself; he can do only what he sees his Father doing, because whatever the Father does the Son also does" (John 5:19).

Jesus, the Savior of the world, could do nothing by Himself? That is an astounding thought. But think:

- When the Father called Jesus to pray, He prayed.
- When the Father called Jesus to go, He went.
- When the Father called Jesus to be moved in healing, He did.
- When the Father called Jesus to die, He gave up His life.

Jesus was always open, always ready, and always willing—to the point of death. Notice Jesus did not suppose *to know*. He supposed to *not know* until the Father showed Him how to go.

Look again at what John 5:19 says: "the Son can do nothing by himself."

Even Jesus did not rely on Himself. This is almost unbelievable. Fully God, Jesus was humble and reliant, obedient to the point of death, and always effective.

If Jesus was reliant on God, how much more should we be? Paul said, "For I decided to know nothing among you except Jesus Christ and him crucified" (1 Cor. 2:2 ESV).

Blank slates are openhearted people in desperate need of the Author's rewrite. To them, the Author is the Source and Finisher of not their own stories but His story, a work playing out in their lives and minds. Jesus said,

> I have come in My Father's name and with His power, and you do not receive Me [your hearts are not open to Me, you give Me

no welcome]; but if another comes in his own name and his own power and with no other authority but himself, you will receive him and give him your approval. (John 5:43 AMPC)

Blank slates say, "Jesus, I need You! I can't do it without You. It is Your power that saves. Jesus, You are the ONLY way! Jesus, You are the truth! Jesus, You are life abundant! Come, Jesus! Come, Holy Spirit! Come. Come. Come. Transform me into Your image by the power of Your grace. You are more than enough, no matter how I feel about me! If You saved the world, You can save me! I believe in You, despite me!"

Blank slates desperately pray more than they endlessly think. Blank slates know Jesus is the only gate to great. Jesus said, "I am the gate for the sheep" (10:7).

How do we come ready to receive Jesus and His work as Author, Source, and Finisher? Blank slates:

1. *Come ready to receive* by hearing, understanding, and perceiving what Jesus is doing and saying to them through the mind of Christ. They are askers, seekers, and knockers. As a result, they find doors open to them.
2. *Don't make the past the final story.* They trust God with tomorrow despite how things looked yesterday.
3. *Get God out of the box and believe He is extraordinarily powerful.*
4. *Pray and ask for help.* They remember, "The heart is deceitful above all things, and desperately sick" (Jer. 17:9 ESV).
5. *Ditch know-it-all, critical, and blaming postures that prohibit growth.*
6. *Don't justify bad behavior but are willing and ready to change course.*

7. *Open their hearts to receive the sifting, shifting, and operation being conducted by the Master Surgeon, the Holy Spirit.* Rather than looking at Scripture and saying, "I know that already," they're open to really knowing God. They welcome Jesus with open arms, just as He died for them with open arms.

The Potential Gain

What is on the other side of a blank slate?
A renewed mind.

> Do not be conformed to this world (this age), [fashioned after and adapted to its external, superficial customs], but be transformed (changed) **by the [entire] renewal of your mind** [by its new ideals and its new attitude], so that you may prove [for yourselves] what is the good and acceptable and perfect will of God, even the thing which is good and acceptable and perfect [in His sight for you]. (Rom. 12:2 AMPC)

Blank-slated minds are renewed. They get new ideals and new attitudes. They get a mind redo. Everything is made over. The Author writes a new story. New attitudes, new mindsets, and new glory make new paths open up to them. They begin to prove what is good and to understand—not by their own minds—the very will of God.

To let go of our own minds is to walk by the mind of Christ.

What is this elusive mind of Christ we keep talking about? First Corinthians 2 tells us:

> But it was to us that God revealed these things by his Spirit. For his Spirit searches out everything and shows us God's deep secrets. No one can know a person's thoughts except that person's own spirit,

and no one can know God's thoughts except God's own Spirit. And we have received God's Spirit (not the world's spirit), **so we can know the wonderful things God has freely given us.**

When we tell you these things, we do not use words that come from human wisdom. Instead, we speak words given to us by the Spirit, using the Spirit's words to explain spiritual truths. But people who aren't spiritual can't receive these truths from God's Spirit. It all sounds foolish to them and they can't understand it, for only those who are spiritual can understand what the Spirit means. Those who are spiritual can evaluate all things, but they themselves cannot be evaluated by others. For,

> **"Who can know the LORD's thoughts?**
> **Who knows enough to teach him?"**

> **But we understand these things, for we have the mind of Christ.** (vv. 10–16 NLT)

The mind of Christ:

1. Searches out things.

2. Reveals things to us by His Spirit.

3. Shows us God's deep secrets.

4. Knows God's deep thoughts and tells them to us.

5. Makes known to us the great things of God.

6. Gives us words from the Spirit.

7. Offers us the Spirit's words to speak spiritual truths.

8. Offers words and wisdom that sound foolish to the world.

9. Speaks our language by giving us understanding.

10. Teaches us the Lord's thoughts.

If we were to *think* like Christ, imagine the immense potential of how much we could *do* and how we could love just like Christ.

Blank-slated minds are primed for renewal. Renewed minds think as Christ thinks, love as He loves, and act as He acts.

As you prepare to go through this book and begin your journey, I encourage you to not come hardened, already knowing everything, assuming your thoughts are correct. Don't come deciding you've already read the Bible and know its stories, verses, and doctrines. Come as a blank slate. Come humble. Come hungry. Come needy. Come ready. Come believing. Come willing. Come expecting God's Word to meet you and renew you. Come anticipating a transformation by God.

Come. Offer yourself as a blank slate to God. Call out to Him. Tell Him your need. Relay the pain. Submit to what He wants to do. Receive His goodness.

Blank slates get new mind narratives written by the Master Author, God Himself.

DECLARATION

I don't have to know it all, because Christ does, and His mind leads me.

Homework

Examine your approach to God. How are you more led by your own thoughts than God's? How do you think you are open—but how might your heart be deceptive? How might you actually be living a closed-up life that's unwelcoming to Christ? How might God be calling you, right now, to let go? To change course?

Note to the Reader

If you haven't received Jesus as your Savior, if you don't know Him in a personal way, if you aren't sure if you will spend eternity with Him, there is more for you, my friend. I want you to receive all that Jesus has for you. I encourage you to make Jesus the Lord of your life by praying this now with me: *Father, I know that I am a sinner. I confess this fact. I can't change me. I need a Savior. I need help. I believe that Jesus died for all my sins. I receive and confess Him as my Lord and Savior. I also ask to be filled with Your Holy Spirit. Thank You, God, for all this. In Jesus's name. Amen.*

────────── **Prayer** ──────────

Father, I can't. I can't do this on my own. My thoughts are not Your thoughts. My ways are not Your ways. Forgive me for my foolishness of mind and for trying to be self-sufficient and independent. Forgive me for doing things my way, on my time, without seeking or yielding to You. I don't want to be a know-it-all. God, I want to know You. I want to be open to Your wisdom. You say You give wisdom generously to those who ask. So, I ask You for it today. Help me to yield to the Holy Spirit, to welcome Jesus in, and to see a new work in my life. I need You, Jesus. I want to see Your renewal in my mind. I welcome You, Jesus. I open myself up to receive from Your Holy Spirit. Come and do a good work in me. In Jesus's name. Amen.

────────── **Free Download** ──────────

To equip you in creating mind change, I've made a "Daily Declarations" sheet. Don't just think of God's Word; own it daily. Visit www.itakethoughtscaptive .com to download.

2

Be a Warrior!

Where the battle rages, there the loyalty of the soldier is proved.

Elizabeth Rundle Charles, *Chronicles
of the Schönberg-Cotta Family*

Normally, when I write a book, I go about things peacefully. I light a fragrant soy candle. I breathe in its floral scent to calm my heart. I place a small vase of colorful flowers on my mahogany table to inspire me. I have my notes in the right order; things are tidy. Coffee, of course, is present. My table is near a big open window. Anytime I take a break, in stillness, I stare out at God's beauty. When doing this, I see a fig tree on the right, tucked close to my windowsill.

This view puts me at rest. But this morning? This morning, although everything was positioned just right, although the house was clean, a mini-war was busting out around me.

Bam! Bam! Bam! Bang! Bang! Bang!

My walls shook. They literally moved!

29

Was my house crashing in on me? I didn't know what was happening at first.

I glanced out my window. Right there, right in my soothing scenery, was a man standing under my fig tree, propped up against my grill.

I was thrown off a tad, though at least I figured out what was happening: today must be the day the crew arrived to work on our siding.

Trying to rise above the situation by ignoring the mayhem, I sat back down by my window to press in to write. I got about a sentence deep, then looked up to think. Lo and behold, the man by the tree was now smoking and staring at me through the window.

How in the world am I supposed to work like this?

Things were invading my space. Trash was being littered outside, on closer inspection. And while this situation certainly wasn't the end of the world, it felt hard with only a short window to write before the kids got home.

What is a woman to do when things invade her space?

I turned up my instrumental music and tried to drown out the invasion. But then things got worse, as they returned my gesture. Obnoxious music began to blast outside. *What was going on? Were they doing this to annoy me?*

My whole workspace—and my mind—was under attack. I couldn't think. I couldn't work. My heart clenched up. My hands tightened. My blood boiled. All I could see and hear was them! Their music. Their smoke. Their presence. Their litter. Their banging . . . over and over again.

I give up, I thought. *I have to stop writing. I can't do this anymore.*

But I knew I could not give up. Why? This issue was symbolic. And it represented the exact mind assault we are all under: outside forces come to disturb our minds.

There is a war raging. But the question is not the war. The question is, How will we go about responding to it?

30

God's Spirit, via the mind of Christ, prompted me to not give up. He made me realize the only way to win a battle is by continuing to fight. The battle is only lost once one quits.

Are you in a battle? You may be waiting and, mentally, that wait is excruciating. You may be hoping that a person will change, and worry is torturing you. You may be on social media facing mounting pressure to be who the world says you should be. You may feel ridiculed by unmet expectations that seem to point a finger at God.

We are all in different types of battles. People litter us with mean words, lies, or verbal attacks. The world labels us *fat* or *poor*. Problems and bills and doctors' diagnoses convince our minds we're doomed. Our walls shake.

The world stares at us. Our problems lurk and wave. The smoke of confusion clouds clarity. Here, it is easy to feel lost and confused on the battlefield of life instead of sure and steady in God's strong tower that's guarded by prayer.

In that moment in my house I knew *I had to fight* for all of us. I knew in that moment my win could become your win too! That it would help us all cease and desist from quitting when the going gets tough.

Fight and resolve rose up in me. This would not be my breakdown moment. It would be my breakthrough moment. By the mind of Christ, I sought God for how to approach this. Scripture says, "Don't act thoughtlessly, but understand what the Lord wants you to do" (Eph. 5:17 NLT). I began praying to discern and understand what God would have me do.

I realized I had the power to turn off the sounds trying to drown out God. I cranked up God-music louder than the offensive music. And, as a result, what blared in the air were messages of "God is bigger, God is stronger, God always overcomes!"

And then I put my head down, stopped looking at those men and all the litter, and wrote this whole section. *Take that, enemy!*

Warriors are not defeated; they turn to God and overcome! They carry on. That's what I did, and that's what you will do too.

Even when, as was the case in my scenario, it feels unorthodox. *Shouldn't I go out there and share the gospel with those men instead? Shouldn't I bring them some water?*

But the point was, what God had for me to do was finish this chapter. He didn't have me outside. He didn't have me quitting and then scrolling on Facebook. He didn't have me texting a friend. His will and purpose for any given moment is more important than my best preconceived notion of what He wants.

The mission we are on, as we take every thought captive, will feel like war sometimes. You will be confronting mental tapes, life strongholds, and decades-long patterns. But when you start the battle resolving to trust God, He will take you through it, whether by foot or by carrying you in His arms.

Knowing it's war is preparatory. It helps you to realize you will need mental determination and fortitude to not quit. It makes you need the power of prayer.

I assure you, you have what it takes to trust God through this process.

The Alternative Path

I could have sulked about the staring, smoking man. I could have whined (which, truth be told, I did a tad when I called my husband to complain, at first). I could have given up, saying, "These workers win. The battle is too much."

But I didn't. I had other assurance.

Christ says, "I have given you authority to trample on snakes and scorpions and to overcome all the power of the enemy; nothing will harm you" (Luke 10:19).

Your battle may be far larger than my mini one. But no matter the size, the authority Christ has given me is assurance I can always lean on. It may be a mind war, but I am not defenseless. I have power through Christ Jesus. It may look impossible, but I serve the Mountain-Maker, not a mountain's worth of issues.

"The Spirit who lives in [me] is greater than the spirit who lives in the world" (1 John 4:4 NLT).

As a warrior, it is helpful when I remember my big battle is nothing compared to my gigantic God. My big problem is a small hangnail in comparison to His might. My mountain is His mole-hill. If He overcame the world, surely He will help overcome the mind chatter, restlessness, and worry that keep me captive.

We Can't Be Dainty about This

How do we fight? One thing I know is we can't be dainty about it.

We are human, but we don't **wage war** as humans do. We **use God's mighty weapons**, not worldly weapons, **to knock down** the strong-holds of human reasoning and to **destroy** false arguments. We destroy every proud obstacle that keeps people from knowing God. **We capture** their rebellious thoughts and teach them to obey Christ. And after you have become fully obedient, we will punish everyone who remains disobedient. (2 Cor. 10:3–6 NLT)

We must be aggressive. We must take a stand. We must decisively move forward and see through the verbs written in these verses. We must *use* our weapons to *knock down* the strongholds, *destroy* proud arguments, and *capture* rebellious thoughts.

Jesus has given us what we need to win. But notice . . . *we* must act to take thoughts captive.

Who does the fighting work belong to? *Us.*

This is not a passive fight; be prepared, my friend. It is an active one.

Who, Me? Yes, You!

The Lord turned to [Gideon] and said, Go in this your might, and you shall save Israel from the hand of Midian. Have I not sent you?

> Gideon said to Him, **Oh Lord, how can I deliver Israel?** Behold, my clan is the poorest in Manasseh, and I am the least in my father's house. (Judg. 6:14–15 AMPC)

How many of us talk to ourselves like Gideon did? *I am the least. I am not capable, not able, too poor, not smart enough. I am this. I am that. I have issues. My past proves I can't.*

How many of us disqualify ourselves and run away afraid? How many of us look in the mirror and doubt what we see? How many of us believe our future is based on what we have or don't have in the natural?

Gideon felt unsure about himself. And, worst of all, in the face of his self-doubt, God was about to strip Gideon. Soon Gideon wouldn't be able to rely on his own strength nor his vast army's. God was about to dwindle his army from twenty-two thousand to a measly three hundred.

> So he brought the people down to the water, and the LORD said to Gideon, "You shall separate everyone who laps the water with his tongue as a dog laps, as well as everyone who kneels down to drink." Now the number of those who lapped [the water], putting their hand to their mouth, was three hundred men, but all the rest of the people kneeled down to drink water. And the LORD told Gideon, "With the three hundred men who lapped I will rescue you, and will hand over the Midianites to you. Let all the other people go, each man to his home." (7:5–7 AMP)

What did Gideon think as he saw his vast army dwindle down to only three hundred fighters? How did he feel as he saw his army looking like dogs as they lapped up water?

The process of dying to our own way is painful. But the resurrection life we gain by following God's way is fruitful. There is no doubt Gideon had to die to his way to become alive to God's victory. This stripping had to happen. Supernatural victory is not achieved by human, natural means.

In the end Gideon, the warrior who did things *God's way*, won the war. He made the whole Midianite army take flight by the power of God's might. But if he had let his small manpower destroy his faith? If he had given up or given in to defeat? If he hadn't trusted God despite how he and his army looked? What would have become of Gideon?

Often it is hard to see things get stripped from us and painful to give up our expectations for how things should play out. Often it is difficult to feel weak and in need. I get it.

I've made many attempts to buoy myself up with achievements, worldly goods, and appearances. And after all this, I can 100 percent say it is the goodness of God to remove or strip anything I rely on more than Him. I am more secure on what feels like shaky ground, because it is really solid rock. It is a foundation of Christ, not my own (no matter how secure my buoys try to make me feel).

A wobbly, floating plank in the water that has God's power under it is steadier than the most solid, rock-steady ground we can build by our own merit. To trust God in awkwardness is a setup to see God move.

That's the thrill. That's the joy of seeing God. That's the trust we can rely on more than what we see. That's the substance of things unseen (aka *faith*).

It wasn't Gideon's large army that was needed to win. It was God's way and God's power. Likewise, it is not our vast intellect, history, appearance, reputation, material goods, or good feelings about ourselves that will make us win but rather God's way and God's power behind us, under us, and around us.

Real warriors who take thoughts captive find God's firm ground, no matter how shaky it feels. They know bad circumstances are bound to be big breakthroughs with God on their side. Beyond disbelief they discover lands of hope and life.

God showed up for Gideon. He will show up for you too. You have an even better covenant, through Christ, than Gideon had. Imagine that!

Let go and let God lead you. Give up and give in to God. There is no advancing troop that can take down a force surrendered to God. Surrender. That's how you win. Obey. That is how you take back the enemy's ground.

It's okay to have no way, to be clueless about how you will do it, to wonder how you will come out the other side. These are great feelings and thoughts! It means you are trusting beyond yourself.

It's okay to sit there with your hands up in the air saying, "I have nothing, God." This reliance is where God advances and helps. This surrender is where our story becomes about His glory more than our smarts, wisdom, power, intellect, or background.

Sometimes the best fight is to give up the fight—then God supernaturally fights on our behalf. He did that with Jesus, who gave up His life on the cross and surrendered to God's redemptive plan— and was resurrected. Giving up is a victory strategy. When we trust God, we make way for Him to move, and He takes over.

Tips for Arming Up and Waging War

When the posture of our hearts as we fight is giving in to God's way, how do we endure as we fight the battle to take every thought captive? There are three wise things to do: know our enemy, combat enemy snakes, and remember who *always* wins the war.

Know Our Enemy

In biblical times, the Romans set the model for what it looked like to take someone captive. Using their authority, when they saw an enemy, they forcefully took that offending enemy down. History shows they were ruthless, unafraid to use brute force, and unrivaled in mental focus. They:

1. Knew who the enemy was.
2. Didn't question the plan to take the enemy captive.
3. Violently took the enemy down without issue.

In ancient battles captured enemy soldiers were either executed or enslaved. . . . Methods of execution included beheading, strangling, being cast from a great height, being buried alive, drowning, death by beast, and crucifixion. . . . Whipping and fines were the most common punishments. Wooden shoes were sometimes placed on the feet of prisoners, making escape difficult. An enslaved person could be forced to carry a piece of wood around their neck that stated their crime.[1]

Although we do not treat people with Roman brutality, because we treat people with love, we also must remember: "our struggle is not against flesh and blood, but against the rulers, against the authorities, against the powers of this dark world and against the spiritual forces of evil in the heavenly realms" (Eph. 6:12). In this, we do brutally—and at all costs—take down the enemy's schemes and approaches. Likewise, we take down any thoughts that rise up as antagonists of Christ Jesus. "We take captive every thought to make it obedient [a slave] to Christ" (2 Cor. 10:5).

We don't do this on defense. We move on offense. No one has ever won a game by playing only defense, without offense. We must know our enemy, know our approach, and be willing to be as violent toward demonic and flesh-centric thoughts as we are when a mosquito lands on our arm ready to bite.

Combat Enemy Snakes

About two months ago, I had a dream in which a snake kept bothering me. I tried to take my journals, in which I wrote Bible verses, and put them on top of the snake, but the snake kept coming out, rising above them. That escapee snake slithered all over my house. I told my husband that we should nail that snake to the wall; however, instead of doing that, we kept the snake as a pet. We fed it, the kids cared for it, and we lived with it.

I can't help but think that many of us have snaky thoughts we keep as pets. These thoughts can often be caused by snaky things. Maybe we're reading a salacious book or watching a show on TV that gets us thinking a certain way. Maybe the news is making us fearful. Maybe that one friend who gossips is making our minds critical. We are hanging out with snakes.

Rather than taking them out, violently nailing them to the cross, we keep them around. We feed them and say, "This must be part of my life." We begin to own, accept, normalize, and expect that mindset.

We have a pet.

The snake we feed grows. Then it bites us, just like it did in my dream.

What are you feeding your mind? What things are filling you? Is your mind full of messages of faith, hope, and love? Or is it speaking fear, death, and nervousness?

What you feed grows.

At one point in my dream, I threw salt on the snake. It seemed like a good idea. But then the snake became large and inflamed, with hornlike sides. It was furious.

Many of us throw a little salt on bad thoughts and call it a day! We don't endure in the fight. Instead we act gingerly, and the enemy's lies grow bigger. Yet we should be moving into hand-to-hand combat and nailing that beast to the wall!

"The Son of God appeared for this purpose, to *destroy the works of the devil*" (1 John 3:8 AMP). As Jesus was nailed to the cross, so was the enemy's endgame. We, too, destroy the works of the enemy by nailing and removing thoughts that are disobedient to Christ Jesus.

No compromise. No excuses. We do it with violence and with vigilance. "And from the days of John the Baptist until now the kingdom of heaven suffereth violence, and the violent take it by force" (Matt. 11:12 KJV).

Don't hang out with pet vices, habits, sin, lures, temptations, or devils anymore. Kill what needs to be killed. Sure, your flesh may die, but your spirit will feel alive.

What lure, sin, or deception do you need to put to death today?

Remember Who Always Wins the War

When I was younger, I felt comfort in scary movies by knowing the protagonist of the story was going to end up okay. If I knew how the story would end, I could have peace in the process.

Friend, we know how the story ends: Jesus wins. "And they have defeated [the enemy] by the blood of the Lamb and by their testimony. And they did not love their lives so much that they were afraid to die" (Rev. 12:11 NLT).

It is important to remind yourself, *You are not going down. You are not going to die. You are going to live forever!*

How can the enemy ever come against this? And not only this but the One who lives and reigns? He intercedes for us (Heb. 7:25). He advocates for us (1 John 2:1). He empathizes with our struggles. There is nothing we are going through that Jesus doesn't understand. He knows.

> No temptation has overtaken you that is not common to man. God is faithful, and he will not let you be tempted beyond your ability, but with the temptation he will also provide the way of escape, that you may be able to endure it. (1 Cor. 10:13 ESV)

You are not alone. You can endure the process of taking every thought captive, of beholding God and becoming like Christ. Best of all, no matter what sort of mess you may find yourself in, there is always a door of escape.

What does all this mean? It means we *endure*. It means we *win*. It means we carry on and get the prize. It means we let Christ's thoughts become our thoughts, His love become our love, and His acts become our acts—so much so that we begin to win wars we never thought we would fight. And thereby we get spoils we never thought we would own!

We "fight the good fight of the faith" (1 Tim. 6:12).

I have fought the good fight, I have finished the race, I have kept the faith. Henceforth there is laid up for me the crown of righteousness, which the Lord, the righteous judge, will award to me on that day, and not only to me but also to all who have loved his appearing. (2 Tim. 4:7–8 ESV)

✠ DECLARATION ✠

I will fight the good fight of faith and will carry on until I meet Jesus!

Homework

Begin a journal, writing down your daily thoughts for one week. Jump-start this effort by using the Daily Thought Tracker in the appendix. Observe your thoughts without judgment or criticism.

Prayer

Father, give me strength. All strength comes from You, and none comes apart from You. I need an infusion of fresh faith so I can walk this walk with You and by You and through You. Make me into a warrior. Make me persevere and endure. Make me strong in the power of Your might. I want to be changed. I hunger and thirst to be like You. I desire to see a new thing. I thank You that You are faithful. Your name is faithful and true. I can trust You. Lead me in Your ways of waging war. Help me not to fight people but to take up my war against the powers and principalities that are behind their actions. Help me to take down strongholds that may have a stronger hold than You in my life. Lead me in all Your ways, open my heart, and let me welcome Jesus into all my ways. In Jesus's name. Amen.

3

Believe You're Worthy of a Changed Mind

A woman in her glory . . . knows in her quiet center where God dwells that he finds her beautiful, has deemed her worthy, and in him, she is enough.

John Eldredge, *Captivating*

How many of us know a person who cannot receive a good word?

You say, "You look beautiful today. I love your free and wavy hair."

They answer, "No, my hair is huge. The humidity makes me look like Orphan Annie."

Because this person doesn't feel good about themselves they can't receive your compliment; they don't believe it. They shut it down. They feel unworthy. They block and deny it. Insecurity makes it difficult for them to believe anything good about themselves.

If they did receive your words, though, they might experience something deep and intimate. They might go home, look at themselves in the mirror, and consider themselves afresh. They might decide, *Wow, my friend was right. I am free. My hair is a picture of who I am. God made me like this on purpose, because it is who He has called me to be. I am a person who brings freedom. As other people see my wild hair, I release others to be themselves too. Maybe I am not unworthy or ugly.*

By not receiving any complimentary words, however, this individual shuts down this sort of opportunity. I know I've done so in the past. When I had an eating disorder in college, every word of goodness went right over my head. I didn't feel worthy of anything good, including food. I ate hollowed-out everything bagels and wanted to torture myself for being bad. I believed I deserved pain.

People who believe they are unworthy tend to hurt themselves. An internal punisher says, *You're not worthy of anything better. You deserve pain. You're bad.* They won't receive life and have no grace for themselves. They may hurt their relationships, too, like their marriage, because they feel bad about themselves. Or they may run away from ministry opportunities. They may even keep themselves hidden and dim Christ's light in them.

These choices are tragedies. You can't receive the good God has for you when you're continuously recounting all the ways you're bad.

Imagine I show up on your doorstep, ready to give you a whole basket of fruit. You see me through the window. You hear me knocking, but due to sadness, past hurts, and a whole lot of tapes playing in your head, you don't have the energy to answer the door. So you don't.

To not receive me, to not open the door because of your issues, is to reject me—and the blessings I intend for your life.

Likewise, to reject the fruit of the Holy Spirit (love, joy, peace, patience, kindness, goodness, faithfulness, gentleness, and self-control) that God owns and wants to give you is to shut the door on the King of Kings. We reject Him when we reject what He says about us. We shut the door in His face when we think His love for us is a generality. To reject God is to reject change for the better. Blocking the goodness of God leads to dejection of heart. We do not get what He knows we need.

How can you receive peace if you won't accept it? How can God give you greater levels of love if you're consumed about your past and what other people have done? How can you be an encourager if you will not receive God's encouragement for you? How can you receive God's mind renewal if you aren't willing to let God in to do something new?

- Do you, even on small levels, reject love?
- Do you reject the help God is giving you because you don't feel good enough? Do you reject your spouse's help or wisdom?
- Do you put yourself down with words like, *I'm a loser. I'm a no-good nothing. I'm worthless?* Do you find it hard to believe that you are God's masterpiece?
- Do you say to yourself, *God can't use me because I haven't been good enough or perfect enough?* Do you feel you have to earn God's love or warrant it with big sacrifices?
- Do you think, *God is angry at me and will withhold good things, His presence, and help?*
- Do you sling words of self-criticism and critique at yourself, like, *Shape up! Get it together! What is wrong with you?*
- Do you internally believe, *God won't transform my mind; that's not for the likes of me?*

I did all these things. I could not receive because I felt horrible about me. I wanted to hurt me because I was so angry at me. *Why am I not a better person? Why don't I do better? I have to earn love to receive it.*

After suffering through my eating disorder, I learned that we either receive God's help or hide away, give up, erect walls, injure others, and move toward a slow and painful death. The wages of sin are death (Rom. 6:23).

Praise God, He saved me from that pit one cool fall night. I'd eaten nothing that day. Faint of mind and disoriented because I hadn't really eaten that whole week, I decided *I had to run!* So I put my sneakers on and got going. It would be three miles, as usual. I passed through my college campus and headed into the dense woods. I could hear the trees swaying. The cool wind hit my goose-bumped arms. I felt tired and weak. But I could do this. I pressed through, telling myself, *You have to, Kelly.* I tried to shove out of my mind the fact that earlier today, my sorority sisters confronted me about my lack of eating and my desire to only eat vegetable stir-fry once in a while. I told them they were 100 percent wrong and shouldn't talk to me that way.

That didn't matter now. Now I was running. I was going to fix myself and do better, look better. I pressed into the heart of the woods. I wanted to fall on the ground but something stopped me dead in my tracks.

I knew it was God. Standing there, on that woody path, I felt the real presence of God surround me.

I'm pretty sure I started to cry. And then I felt what seemed like a nudge on my heart, accompanied by a clear message within my mind, saying something like, *Kelly, you can either come to Me and follow Me, or you can continue to go on your path and die.*

That was an awakening. Self-centeredness, rooted in selfishness, is self-ruin. I knew I would have to get out of my mind to get into His.

My feelings of inferiority, insecurity, and unworthiness would have to die in order for me to really live—in Christ. All along, I had been trying to kill the wrong thing. I was trying to physically kill what I hated about myself, but what Jesus wanted to put to death was my self-hate, so I could find His love for me, how He defined me, and my worth according to Him. And so I could permanently live in that space with Him.

While I was running away, Jesus was saying, *Come to Me.* And He's always saying this, as evidenced by how He died on the cross, arms wide open. This picture of Him on the cross reminds us He is always saying, *You are welcome to come to Me.*

My goodness now is not about me; it is about Him. He always wants me. He has already chosen me. His grace is enough to bring me to His throne.

"The Spirit and the bride say, 'Come!'" (Rev. 22:17). And I did come to Jesus. I got help. I was rescued by the King of Kings, and, amazingly (unlike most sufferers of eating disorders), I was healed. Jesus healed my unworthiness so I could receive His worthiness.

Many of us have silently decided, *I'm unworthy!* We think a strong and confident mind is for other saints. For those holier than us. We think we will always feel dejected, like a loser, or left out.

The issue with this is we can't believe in our minds what we can't conceive we're worthy of. Doubt will say, *God couldn't really love me like this. I'm not good enough. I'm junk. I messed up too much.* Thoughts like these will block out God's redeeming and all-surpassing love and truth.

We can't own what we won't receive. All the spiritual blessings Jesus has already blessed us with (Eph. 1:3), we will refuse and not own. We will deem our perception of self higher than His.

Yet when we receive God's love, it changes our minds. Here, our thoughts get rewired and hope returns. This is mind renewal, when His thoughts about us becomes our thoughts about us. It is when His love not only works through us but works in us. It is when we receive Him as our security rather than giving in to insecurity. Only then can we truly love others.

"We love because he first loved us" (1 John 4:19).

We can never give to others what we ourselves don't first own.

We're Unworthy!

God uses unworthy people—who gain worth through Christ Jesus. Let's take a look.

John the Baptist

John hesitated to baptize Jesus. "John *tried to prevent Him*, saying, 'I need to be baptized by You, and are You coming to me?'" (Matt. 3:14 NKJV).

Can you imagine? In that moment, John rejected Jesus. This is a calling one could only hope to live for! What a high honor! Yet John almost missed the blessing because of his feelings of unworthiness. Likely John thought, *Who, me? I can't.* In essence, John was saying his inferiority trumped the sovereignty of the Savior's plan. That he had the right to halt what Jesus was doing.

Whoa. Can you see how insecurity and feelings of *I'm unworthy* can also be pride? Here John was face-to-face with probably the greatest calling of his life, certainly the greatest Person in his life, and he wanted to shut down this moment. He was prepared to stop God's very will in its tracks, because of what? Flesh.

Is pride trying to stop *you* from receiving what Jesus has for you?

Many of us have humility and pride backward. It isn't prideful to think we are worthy; it is prideful to tell Jesus His good plan is unworthy of us. It isn't prideful to be honored and used by Jesus; it is prideful to shy away and use so-called humility as a bunker for fear. Jesus, no matter how big or small we may feel, makes us worthy. He deserves our complete submission and utter reception, whether we are lifted up or cast low. It is not about where we stand or how we stand (high or low); it is who we serve!

The idea is to move this worthy/unworthy dilemma out of the way. It is to remove "us" from the equation. It is usually not that we think less of ourselves but less often about ourselves.

How did Jesus reply to John's self-focus?

46

"But Jesus answered [John] and said to him, 'Permit it to be so now, for thus it is fitting for us to fulfill all righteousness.' Then he allowed Him" (v. 15 NKJV).

Jesus healed John the Baptist, basically saying, "Move yourself aside, John." In essence, He was conveying, "Get your flesh out of My way, John. It's not about you."

John obeyed.

We move our flesh out of the way of what God is doing, and God gets His glory. It is not about us. It is about Him. We are simply worthy because, thanks to Jesus, we have His worth now. Apart from Him we're nothing. But with Him we can do anything (Phil. 4:13).

Peter

When Jesus wanted to wash Peter's feet, He "came to Simon Peter, who said to him, 'Lord, are you going to wash my feet?' Jesus replied, 'You do not realize now what I am doing, but later you will understand.' 'No,' said Peter, 'you shall never wash my feet'" (John 13:6–8).

Let this settle in for a minute.

Can you even believe that Peter said, "No, you shall never" to the King of Kings and the Lord of Lords? That's like a three-year-old kid, in all seriousness, ordering the president of the United States, saying, "You will never!" and meaning it. It's almost laughable.

Peter, a grown man, said this to the God of all the universe.

To stop God's plan due to our own sense of self can be both disobedience and rebellion. Sure, feeling unworthy and sinful and horrible about yourself looks good and religious at face value, but is it what God wants?

Do you walk in pride yet call it religious meekness? Over the years, I have heard some pronouncements like, "Woe is me. I am a sinner."

I will admit, I have wondered, *What are they really saying?* Are they truly humble, or are they counting themselves out? Choosing not to believe God for greater things? Trying to earn something from God? Or loudly megaphoning their low and measly humility to look religious?

Of course, I can't judge because I don't know their hearts . . . and they are right, because without Jesus we are all just horrible sinners. But also true is the fact that because of Him we're redeemed! By grace, God calls us higher than an all-consuming, flesh-centric, self-berating sin focus. Thank God. I am more than my sin, and so are you.

Our truest identity is *Christ*. It is this identity that has personally changed me from hating myself and wanting to kill myself to feeling full of Jesus—His love and His thoughts—more often than not!

The bottom line, here, as it relates to Peter is Jesus wanted Peter not only to receive a foot washing but fresh humility. Receiving is humility. To receive is to understand God as the Complete Provider . . . as the Ultimate Source. Here, you know that you know all your fountains, all your hope, all your life is in Him. He is all you need.

Humility does not fight the Maker of the Universe.

Jesus answered Peter, "Unless I wash you, you have no part with me" (v. 8). That's a big response from Jesus. And a scary one, when we really think about it.

Like Peter, we will have no part in the mind of Christ without receiving His thoughts, His heart, His washing, and His mind for us.

Will we be receivers, or will we be deniers because we are so bent on keeping a flesh-centric sin identity?

None of us are worthy without the saving blood of Jesus, but all of us are worthy because of it. Will we take and eat His body, no matter how arrogant and self-indulgent it feels, or will we turn away, declaring we don't deserve it? Will we receive His helping hand or bat it away? Will we hear His voice in the wilderness, or will we keep running to our own demise? One choice connects to the heart and mind of Christ, and the other leads to a prideful death.

There is no mind renewal without receiving.

Receive This!

Receiving means sitting and pondering. It means taking a truth and letting it become part of you. Chewing on it. Asking God about it. Seeing it on you. Receiving goes beyond the mind, directly to the heart.

Receive this: God thinks good thoughts about you. Often. His thoughts are lasting and not wavering. He keeps track of your hard days, He understands you, He notices all things about you, He is jealous for you, He wants you, and, before time began, He chose you for a specific purpose.

Write these verses out in your journal. Ask the Father to reveal, by His Spirit, what they mean for your life.

> How precious also are Your thoughts to me, O God!
> How great is the sum of them! (Ps. 139:17 NKJV)

> The counsel of the LORD standeth for ever, **the thoughts of his heart** to all generations. (33:11 KJV)

> You keep track of all my sorrows.
> You have collected all my tears in your bottle.
> You have recorded each one in your book. (56:8 NLT)

> Even from far away **you understand** my motives. (139:2 NET)

> You know when I sit and when I rise;
> **you perceive** my thoughts from afar. (139:2)

For the LORD your God is a consuming fire, a jealous God. (Deut. 4:24)

But you are a chosen people, a royal priesthood, a holy nation, God's special possession, that you may declare the praises of him who called you out of darkness into his wonderful light. (1 Pet. 2:9)

He has saved us and called us to a holy life—not because of anything we have done but because of his own purpose and grace. (2 Tim. 1:9)

Do you see what I see? There is no worthlessness when you place your mind under the lordship of Jesus. The Father sent His Son for you.

No one bothers with a rescue mission for something unwanted. You wouldn't dive down to the ocean floor to rescue a painting from the depths unless you knew it was worth a lot. Jesus came to the depths of decrepit earth to rescue you. This says something about you.

When you receive your worth in Christ, you are receiving His mind toward you. The goal is that His mind become yours. I pray this is beginning to happen, by His power, right now for you.

What Helped Me See My Worth

What changed me from a starving, mentally challenged individual to a woman on fire and full of purpose for God was not memorizing Bible verses but soaking them into my very being. Receiving Christ in me.

This is how I became a truly new creation, wholly made over. My whole world got a new glint. Because of this, I saw myself through new eyes. Rather than seeing *Kelly is a garbage bag of sin*, I began to recognize Jesus living in me and working in me from the inside out.

In this, I could let go of my self-centered and critical self-focus. I could acknowledge Jesus.

Or do you not realize this about yourselves, that **Jesus Christ is in you**? (2 Cor. 13:5 ESV)

In the same way, count yourselves dead to sin but **alive to God in Christ Jesus**. (Rom. 6:11)

It is **no longer I who live, but Christ who lives in me.** And the life I now live in the flesh I live by faith in the Son of God, who loved me and gave himself for me. (Gal. 2:20 ESV)

Therefore, if anyone is in Christ, **he is a new creation.** The old has passed away; behold, **the new has come.** (2 Cor. 5:17 ESV)

How can I be hard on myself when I am submitting, yielding, and obeying He who is in me? The shift from me to Him relieved me of self-focus and self-punishing ways. How can I punish Jesus in me when He has already been punished so much?

Now I recognize the importance of putting on my new nature every day, every minute, so I can submit and yield to the mind of Christ. Then the patient, kind, gentle, and faith-giving presence of Jesus shows up organically. I no longer have to constantly track my sin identity and walk in constant fear management. All that is foolishness in light of His glory and grace, which I keep returning to. I've come to realize Jesus doesn't look at me and see my dysfunction; Jesus looks at me and sees His reflection, the image of Christ in me. That is consoling.

Wearing the mind of Christ by the power of Christ in us is a practical and effective way to renew our minds.

What changed me from wanting to die, being mean to my kids and hating myself for it, constantly criticizing people, being ultracompetitive with other women, being horridly selfish, getting all caught up in a million feelings of inadequacy, suffering from anxiety, and regretting the past was embracing Christ in me.

Join me in receiving and declaring helpful truths like these:

I am not my sin!

I walk by the power of Christ in me.

I am dead to sin and alive to Christ.

It is no longer I who live, but Christ who lives in me!

I am not led by the flesh, which is death, but by the Spirit. I walk into life and peace.

When I declare these truths, I give up to Jesus and give in to the way He leads me to love, helps me to see people in need, and brings me beyond my own world. I yield to Christ in me and His love that died to get out through me. I live the Word of God rather than just read it.

You can do this too. Write down those verses. Own them. Absorb them. Speak them aloud. Don't let go of them until you receive Jesus this way. Until you know He has ownership and you are His possession (Eph. 1:13–14).

Another practical tool for accomplishing this is to listen to an audio version of the Bible and play Colossians 3; Romans 6; Romans 8; Galatians 2; and 2 Corinthians 5 on repeat, again and again. Bathe in living water. Let the Word of God, the thoughts of Christ, go low to wash the dirt of insecurity and unworthiness right off your feet.

Take the Living Word at His Word. Believe it at all costs. Hold it in the highest esteem. Then more authority will come on you and more unworthiness and doubt will fall off you. As Billy Graham once prayed, "Father, I am going to accept this as Thy Word—by faith! I'm going to allow faith to go beyond my intellectual questions and doubts, and I will believe this to be Your inspired Word."[1]

Only when we take God at His Word will the Word take hold of us. Only when His Word dwells in our hearts does it become our dwelling. The Word is not read and passed over. The Word is captured and held in a precious box, like one that holds fine jewelry. We gaze at it so much His Word becomes our word. When His words are the words we are speaking to ourselves and to others—words of love, hope, and life—we can surely know our minds are successfully walking out the renewal process.

How This Shapes Up Practically in a Life

You may have been married three times. You may have made a lot of parenting mistakes. You may be that person who can't hold a job. You may be someone who has slept around. You may have foolishly wasted your material resources. You may have made a million bad choices. You may have deeply and heartfeltly repented.

Regardless, I want to drive home this point: You are not your sin. Christ's ability to save is too complete to let you be your sin; you are a child of the King of Kings. You also are not your past. Nor are you a victim. You aren't fighting to *get* good from God—you *already have everything* in Christ Jesus. In fact, God so wants you that He put His very own Holy Spirit inside you. He wants to be near you.

Always ponder His goodness rather than your badness. Then you will gain confidence to:

- Believe the best about what God is doing in and through you.
- Hope and pray again for things you once desired.
- Give yourself the grace Jesus paid for.
- Trust Jesus wants to help you.
- Receive the nudges, promptings, and leadings of God as you study and live out His Word and the material in this book.
- Go out and do the things you've only dreamed of doing.
- Enjoy God and His Word again.

Then, naturally, you will start to do things like:

- Saying no to spending time with people who put you down, antagonize Jesus, or criticize you.
- Hanging out with people who encourage you.

- Honoring yourself with your words rather than putting yourself down.
- Taking care of yourself through healthy sleeping, eating, and exercising.
- Deciding not to be used and abused anymore.
- Going after what God really has for you—without guilt.
- Setting boundaries.

Mind renewal brings life refreshment! See Christ in you. Think upon His love for you. Know who His Word says you are. Look at the world through Him and His Word. Protect these things as sacred.

Jesus didn't die for someone unworthy of His love. My friend, you are wholly, entirely, completely, and amazingly worthy of His love.

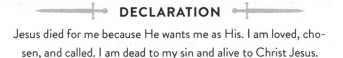

DECLARATION

Jesus died for me because He wants me as His. I am loved, chosen, and called. I am dead to my sin and alive to Christ Jesus.

Homework

Draw a line down the center of a piece of paper. Write on one side of the line a list of every way you feel unworthy. On the other side, search the Word (use Google if you need to) for verses that speak the opposite of what you wrote on that list (item by item). Take one verse a day and journal on it. Make some verbal declarations that you can begin to proclaim over yourself. Tell your mind what to believe. Your mind listens to what you have to say, and it agrees with what you think. The more you tell yourself truth, the more your mind will come to believe it.

———— Prayer ————

Father, I thank You that You loved me so much that You gave Your Son for my life. Thank You for saving me. I ask You to help me know my worth in You. Help me to put on my new identity. May I remember who I am in You. May I honor myself and the mind of Christ in me. May I treasure You in the temple called me! In Jesus's name. Amen.

———— Free Download ————

Download more declarations that you can speak over yourself to feel your value and worth at www.itakethoughtscaptive.com.

PART 2

Be Strong of Heart, Be Strong of Mind

4

Develop a Heart of Gold

Anticipate that God will start working with you and drawing you to an intimate love relationship that is real and personal. When the love relationship is right, God will be free to begin giving you assignments at His initiative.

Henry T. Blackaby, *Experiencing God*

Remember that old game Whack-a-Mole? I played it as a kid. The goal of the game is to hit the plastic mole with a bat. When it pops up through a hole, you're supposed to whack it. But right before you can hit it, the thing disappears and pops up elsewhere. It keeps moving. It pops up from other holes. You whack again. You look from one place to another, trying to chase the thing down. Then it moves again, to another hole. You start sweating. It's hard to keep up with that silly thing.

So it goes with our thoughts. If we address a thought without handling its underlying heart issue, we will play a never-ending game of Whack-a-Mole when we try to take our thoughts captive. We will handle a thought for a moment but still have a lifelong problem that keeps popping up and pestering us. We will keep whacking and getting nowhere.

For instance, you may get beyond the thought that makes you critique a girl's outfit at church only to, a day later on Facebook, size everyone up—their outfits, their words, their ways. You may turn away from drinking for a week and instead resort to online shopping. You may intend to spend time with God by being less distracted with busyness but then get caught up in organizing your home.

Are you chasing moving targets?

I don't know about you, but I don't want to move from one thought-problem to another; I want to handle the problem. I want to nail it, once and for all.

A heart of gold produces thoughts as good as gold.

Heart Matters

I thought this morning, as I looked at my garden, *The right wisdom can make almost anyone good at anything.* With this, I thought, *I can be a decent gardener! How?* I drove to a nursery to purchase a new plant. I asked the expert on staff exactly what soil to use, how wide to make the hole for the plant, and how often to water it. Because of this, I felt confident I'd have a successful garden.

As I figure it, this concept doesn't stop with plants.

I'm sure if I learned the knife skills of sushi chefs, over time I'd prepare sushi masterfully. If I learned ice hockey tricks and applied myself to practicing them, I'd become a good player.

What we care about, we learn about. What we learn, we become good at. What we become good at, if we continue to apply ourselves to it, we become masters over.

We are called to *"Above all else,* guard your heart" (Prov. 4:23). To do this, we must become masters of the heart!

Let's talk about the heart. The heart is not something to ignore. It is the beating lifeblood of our lives. Without it, there is no life.

We can't live with a broken heart. This is why I believe God is sounding an alarm with His words, "Above all else." These words scream, "Hey, YOU! Above all else (hear Me!)—*guard your heart,* already!"

We must guard our hearts. Our lives depend on it. To guard our hearts, we must know more about them and how they work. Let's start the learning process.

1. *Your heart is deceptive.* "The heart is *deceitful above all things* and beyond cure. Who can understand it?" (Jer. 17:9). Your heart, left alone and on its own accord, cannot be trusted. It lies. For instance, have you ever come to realize something about yourself that you didn't before? I realized this past month that I put serving others before serving my family. If you told me I was doing this a couple of weeks ago, I wouldn't have believed you. I probably would have fought you and defended my cause. But, through God's illumination, I got a revelation about the deception in my heart. Might a heart of deception be leading you astray in any way?

2. *Your heart thinks.* "For as he thinketh in his heart, so *is* he" (Prov. 23:7 KJV). You don't think from your mind; you think from your heart. If your heart is off, your course will be off too. Think of a sailboat moving slightly off course. It will end up miles away from its target. It's a big deal to be off course. Our hearts must think right for our thoughts to be right. When our thoughts are right, good destinations come into sight. That's what we want.

3. *Everything you do flows from your heart.* "Above all else, guard your heart, for everything you do flows from it" (4:23). Your heart is the founder of everything, your thoughts manufacture an interpretation from your heart, and your actions and words are the delivery system, sending out whatever began in your heart.

Your heart determines your livelihood. It charts courses. None of us want to find out ten years from now that we are somewhere—but nowhere at all where we wanted to be. That would be a travesty.

The most horrible feeling is to think you're doing good only to realize your protection mechanism, defensiveness, projection, or denial has put you in a place far away from what God sees as good. Or to see everything combust around you when you didn't even realize you were doing anything wrong. That's the worst! I know—I've been there.

The heart can't be trusted. You may think you're okay to skip church for a couple of months but then fall away from God. You may think you're amazingly godly but actually are judgmental and critical rather than loving and hope-filled. You may say you value God but undervalue Him when the rubber meets the road of real-life issues. You may say you rely on God but do everything by your own counsel and wisdom rather than trusting, relying on, and leaning on the mind of Christ. You may say you love God but never spend time with Him. You may say you trust God but worry endlessly. You may say you are a Christian but have no fruit to show for it.

Where might your heart be fooled?

Deluded thinking thinks everything is good—until it really isn't. It thinks it is okay until a bomb explodes that finally wakes the thinker up to the catastrophic reality of what they've ignored for too long.

"Who may ascend the hill of the LORD? Who may stand in His holy place? He who has clean hands and a pure heart, who does not lift up his soul to an idol or swear deceitfully" (Ps. 24:3–4 BSB). God wants the real thing. Authentic hearts. He is 100 percent holy, and so halfway holy is not His highest or best.

Those with pure hearts are the ones who ascend the hill of the Lord. They behold God and become like Him. With this, of course, their minds are renewed and they begin to think more like Jesus thinks. It's natural. We become like the company we keep.

As Our Hearts Go, So Do Our Lives

Bad hearts produce bad things; good hearts produce good things. What begins in the depths of a heart soon plays out in a person's actions.

Take Sue, for instance. Sue is angry inside. People have taken advantage of her generosity in the past. One person even took her money, and instead of using it for the poor and needy as promised, they ran off with it. Sue hasn't forgiven any of these offenders because it is all too upsetting. She's lost thousands of dollars. Now Sue is fed up, bitter, and broken in general.

So, what happens when her friend Joanne asks her to donate money to fund her trip to an orphanage?

Sue goes off and blasts Joanne. She says, "How dare you ask me for money? You have enough money. All you care about is money." She harbors resentment toward her friend. She reacts.

Sue's unforgiving heart produces unbecoming actions.

Whether sourced from unforgiveness, unrepentance, unjust situations, or simply feeling unloved, her heart has made a course for her thoughts. Her words follow suit. And so her friendship with Joanne could be ruined as a result.

Hearts are triggered by stimuli that lead us to an action.

David, in the Bible, had a lustful heart, and he illegally gazed on Bathsheba and produced adultery and murder. Judas had a critical spirit and a greedy heart. He wondered why a woman would pour out her life savings on Jesus's feet, and he produced the ultimate betrayal of Jesus. The Pharisees had pride in their hearts and thought themselves better than Jesus, and they produced distance that kept them from truly knowing the Savior.

Bad hearts produce bad things; good hearts produce good things. Jesus. John the Baptist. The apostle Paul.

A good heart is something God can bless. Take a look at some of the blessings in the Bible directly connected to good hearts:

"And if you love and obey the LORD, you will *live long* in the land the LORD swore to give your ancestors Abraham, Isaac, and Jacob" (Deut. 30:20 NLT).

"If you do this, then the LORD will keep the promise he made to me. He told me, 'If your descendants live as they should and *follow me faithfully with all their heart and soul, one of them will always sit on the throne of Israel'*" (1 Kings 2:4 NLT).

"All in Judah were happy about this covenant, for they had entered into it *with all their heart.* They earnestly sought after God, and they found him. And *the LORD gave them rest* from their enemies on every side" (2 Chron. 15:15 NLT).

Love proves a pure heart. Faithful following, with all our hearts invested in God's plan no matter the cost, makes us take heart. On the flip side, divided loyalty distresses a heart.

Why is a pure heart important to our walk? Imagine a friend you know and trust. Because time has proven this person's heart as one you can trust in your relationship, you can tell this individual almost anything. You can share vulnerable things, right? God trusts those with pure hearts. These are people God reveals Himself to. "Blessed are the pure in heart, for they will see God" (Matt. 5:8).

A pure heart can receive, by its nature, more of God.

Do you have a pure heart? A bless-able heart? A wholly devoted heart?

A *pure heart lives by this*: "And you shall love the LORD your God with all your heart and with all your soul and with all your strength" (Deut. 6:5 NASB).

A *pure heart trusts this*: "But seek first his kingdom and his righteousness, and all these things will be given to you as well" (Matt. 6:33).

A *pure heart receives God's grace*: "Let us draw near with a
true heart in full assurance of faith, with our hearts sprinkled clean from an evil conscience and our bodies washed
with pure water" (Heb. 10:22 ESV).

Again, a pure heart knows God as our Source. It remembers
He is also our Author and Finisher. It receives His sacrifice when
it messes up. More than seeking blessings, it pursues the joy of
knowing God. Blessings are just cherries on top of what God is
already doing. A pure heart is on fire to be closer to God, to do
God's will, and to walk in His ways.

This heart of gold praises, gives thanks to, gives glory to, and
honors the King of Kings. It wants God's honor first. It praises
along with heaven, saying nearly in one accord, "To him who sits
on the throne and to the Lamb be praise and honor and glory and
power, for ever and ever!" (Rev. 5:13).

When a mind gets here—to a place of unadulterated worship
and praise, to a place of overflow of heart, to a place that is gushing
love—*this* is a mile marker of a renewed mind! A heart of gold.
A mind filled and flooded with Christ! This is what we are after.

A heart of gold is one that wholly loves God, first and foremost.
It is all in!

Purified as Gold—What It Looks Like

How are we purified as gold?

God builds character in crucibles. He purifies us as gold so we
have thoughts of gold.

This is so embarrassing to admit, in a way, but I have to confess
that I had a greed problem. I always thought I knew best. Specifically, *I knew* what my husband should do for his business. I thought
I had the best ideas on how to make more money. The best strategy.
I thought I could handle closing deals better than he did. Guess
what happened? Nothing I offered prospered. Ever. Not once. In

fact, my ideas probably did the opposite of prospering. Despite my great sales and marketing background, they fell flat, like a dead tire. Worst of all, I probably drove my husband nuts—for years. So, there's that. I feel horrible about it. The heart is deceptive. What I thought was a good thing to do was actually a horrible thing to do.

"Unless the LORD builds the house, the builders labor in vain" (Ps. 127:1).

God wants pure gold—His own personal glory-gold, not our cheap-imitation version.

Far more, these days, I want to bring praise and glory to the Father. I don't always have to be seen. I don't always have to be the one speaking. I don't always have to have the answers. I stay united, even when I lack.

And this, my friend? This place is a treasure place of freedom, connectedness, and security in Christ.

How do we get to this place?

1. We go through the hard times and learn. God wanted to make my heart pure as gold through the furnace of afflic-tion. For some, this may not be comfortable to talk about. It may seem heavy. It's not as fluffy as some other Chris-tian books where authors use cool words, share cool sto-ries, and keep the topics socially light. But I am not here to please you; I am here to please God. We gain hearts of gold through trial by fire.

So that the tested genuineness of your faith—more precious than gold that perishes though it is tested by fire—may be found to result in praise and glory and honor at the revelation of Jesus Christ. (1 Pet. 1:7 ESV)

2. We set our hearts on the reward of God and consider all other things small in comparison.

For our light and momentary troubles are achieving for us an eternal glory that far outweighs them all. (2 Cor. 4:17)

There is praise and glory and honor that come at the revelation of Jesus. What will this look like—for you and for me? It will look like reward! It will look like everlasting crowns.

The crown of victory (1 Cor. 9:25)

The crown of a soul winner (Phil. 4:1; 1 Thess. 2:19)

The crown of righteousness (2 Tim. 4:8)

The crown of life (James 1:12)

The crown of glory (1 Pet. 5:4)

One day, our crowns will be thrown down at Jesus's feet. Our accomplishments or lack thereof will not be center stage. Jesus will. The same goes today. It is not about our expectations, our desires, our will, or our wants. It is about His glory.

Ultimately, hearts of gold know the highest calling is to bring all praise and all glory to the Savior rather than to the self. They dwell on God rather than dwelling in worry.

Pure hearts are accompanied by minds fixed on heaven. Instead of resorting to worry, apprehension, or anxiety—and therefore picturing worst-case scenarios—they think on heavenly things. They might picture Jesus and the uproariously loud praise for Him that will come from the cloud of witnesses and from the Father—because the King of Kings is getting all His glory. They may think upon the day of Jesus's big return and the whole universe exploding with His glory. Every knee bending. All creation knowing. All people declaring. Every person falling on their face.

Jesus reigning.

A mind seeing a picture like this cannot be worried or anxious or engaging in unhealthy rumination. "You will keep in perfect peace those whose minds are steadfast, because they trust in you" (Isa. 26:3).

God builds character through the crucible of heart-change. It is through fire that our minds are made moldable, changeable, and transformable. When we submit to Jesus in the fire, we become like Him and, naturally, think like Him too.

✦ DECLARATION ✦

I welcome being purified as gold so that I can bring
loads and loads of glory-gold to Jesus.

Homework

"Who may climb the mountain of the LORD? Who may stand in his holy place? Only those whose hands and hearts are pure, who do not worship idols and never tell lies" (Ps. 24:3–4 NLT). Begin to pray this "Heart-Altering Life Prayer" regularly: *Father, give me clean hands and a pure heart, and never let me tell lies. In Jesus's name. Amen.*

Prayer

Father, oh, how I love You. Oh, how I want to glorify You. Oh, how I want Jesus to be high and lifted up. Oh, how I want to be a praise to Your glory. Father, change my heart. Mold it and remake it. Transform it by Your glory and power. For then all my life will change. Give me clean hands and a pure heart. Help me, above all else, to guard my heart. In Jesus's name. Amen.

Free Download

Get three "Start Your Day!" scriptural daily prayers to kick off your morning. Live from a whole heart. Visit www.itakethoughtscaptive.com.

5

Allow Experience
to Transcend Knowledge

We always know when Jesus is at work because He produces in the commonplace something that is inspiring.

Oswald Chambers, *My Utmost for His Highest*

Thoughts are usually sourced from experiences. We remember things that happen to us. Then thoughts generated from these experiences form life outlooks. This is important to know because experiences, in our minds, have greater weight than things we're told. Consider:

- An experience of a sunburn will remind us to put on sunscreen more than being told about the merits of sunscreen application.
- An experience of pain in relationship will make us ask ourselves, *Can I trust this person?* more than a person telling us, "Mishandled trust is hard to gain back."

- Repeated experiences of a parent lying to us transcends their instruction to "Never tell lies."

What experiences have shaped your thoughts? Your beliefs? Your outlook?

Experiences create go-to emotional responses. We may not even realize we are responding based on an old experience. Conclusions we've drawn can speak louder than even truth speaks—and we read people's minds, make assumptions, and just figure people are doing what happened to us in the past. All this can drown out the still, small voice of God.

When this happens, we come to see what we expect to see.

One person sees a six. Another sees a nine.

Why? Experiences.

What we've seen in the past often shapes what we see in the present. When we form beliefs, we create neural pathways in our minds. Cognitive bias makes us search out and confirm what we already think. The person who sees a six will seek out and see more sixes. The one who sees a nine will seek and find more nines. Each act is based on their previously received information, right or wrong.

We don't want poor past experiences to dictate our future. Neither do we want mountaintop moments to shape how we live,

lest we fall into the other pit, which is called *pride* and *ego*. The ultimate goal of our hearts is to experience God in such a way that, by His grace and power, He changes the neural firing in our minds. Only when we are transformed through experiencing the light of God's presence are we conformed to His image and made into something entirely new.

Then, rather than becoming another mouthpiece for the hype of this world, a rerun of the national news, a gossiper like those we hang out with, a victim of the past, or someone living out a vain worry we've conjured up in our minds, we will see Jesus and become like Jesus. We will know Jesus and know He is wholly making us over. Just like He made fishermen into apostles, Saul the persecutor into Paul the missionary, and Simon into Peter. As you will come to see, we are transformed, experientially, in light of His glory and grace.

"Knowing" Changes a Mind

To experience something is to make something real. People can tell you about Paris, but until you go and taste a chocolate croissant and stand before the Eiffel Tower, the city is just a picture in a magazine, not a personal reality. People can explain what being married is like, but until you tie the knot there's no really knowing what it's like to live with a spouse. People can tell you that children should never watch TV, but until they've spent twelve hours with a cranky two-year-old, there's no judging.

Experiencing is knowing. One might understand concepts in thought but not apprehend them until they've experienced them in real life. Experience solidifies knowing.

Even science backs this up: "Neuroplasticity, also known as brain plasticity, is a term that refers to the brain's ability to change and adapt as a result of experience."[1] The mind is malleable, changeable. The more we experience something, the more a new pathway cuts through our stagnant minds to a new place—away from the old mind-ruts we created. This is encouraging. The more we experience new things, the more we have new thoughts that create new neural pathways to new go-to ways of thinking.

The Greek word *ginosko*, used many times in the Bible, is all about knowing through experience. *Ginosko* translates as "to learn, to know, to perceive, to feel, to become known, to understand, to become acquainted."[2]

Ginosko is the sort of knowing where you don't just see the brownies on the counter but you *ginosko* know those brownies. How? You've bit into one. You've felt that gooeyness, that crunchy outside and soft inside. You remember the taste exploding in your mouth. You also know it is probably dark chocolate with extra chocolate chips, and it must have been baked today because it is so mouthwateringly delicious. This is knowing that brownie by *ginosko* experience—and you know it is heavenly. You also know, undoubtedly, that you want more.

Through experiential, *ginosko* knowing, we come to truly know God and ourselves—beyond what we *thought* we knew. *Ginosko* knowing transcends what we thought we *had to* believe, what doubts held us back, what people demanded we think, and what assumptions we made up in our minds. It makes a theory into a reality. It makes truth solid. It makes the Word of God alive.

All this transfigures us from *who we thought we were* into *who God says we are*. Remember when Jesus was transfigured? When "his face shone like the sun, and his clothes became as white as the light" (Matt. 17:2)?

In light of the fullness of God's glory, Jesus was revealed as He truly was—and He shone bright. The disciples had an experiential, *ginosko*, come-to-know-Jesus-as-God moment. No one could deny it. It was happening before their very eyes! And then the Father spoke from "a bright cloud [that] overshadowed them, and a voice from the cloud said, 'This is my dearly loved Son, who brings me great joy. Listen to him'" (v. 5 NLT).

The disciples were moved into a deeper knowing. They now *truly ginosko knew* what they once *thought* they knew. They saw Jesus as He was known to the Father.

We don't just seek to know God to gain Bible knowledge, learn some trivia, or look religious. We know God to be changed into His image. We are after a *ginosko* knowing of God that's true and deep. Experiential knowing brings about the transformation and transfiguration that make us become more like Him. Think more like Him. Talk more like Him. Walk more like Him. Love more like Him. Reach the devil-oppressed more like Him. Heal more like Him. See more like Him. Lay down our lives more like Him.

All of it is in Him, through Him, and by Him—by knowing Him. Really, deeply, intimately, relationally knowing Him in every part of our lives. Take a look at how God encourages us to experience Him:

> May Christ through your faith [actually] dwell (settle down, abide, make His permanent home) **in your hearts!** May you be rooted deep in love and founded securely on love, **that you may have the power** and be strong to apprehend and grasp with all the saints [God's devoted people, **the experience of that love**] what is the breadth and length and height and depth [of it]. (Eph. 3:17–18 AMPC)

Let's pause here. Did you hear what I heard? Through Christ's residential indwelling, we become *founded securely* in His love. This is how separating ourselves from the world happens. We become so established in God's love—we gain so much experience of it—that we get disconnected from everything else.

This power is not a figurative power; it is transforming power. But notice what is needed—what we are required to carry—to access this love-power. FAITH. We have to have faith to enter God's love, to receive His love, to believe His love, and to radically experience His love.

So, do you believe God wants to meet you?

Some come to the Bible as a duty; others come to it as a play-ground of God's delight and a place to encounter His heart, which is about to fill theirs.

The difference is dimensions apart. One plays in a field of head knowledge; the other digs into the dirt and finds treasures and levels of God's amazing grace, power, and a fullness they never imagined could be found.

Do you have faith? Do you believe God's love for you is powerful enough to renew you and remold you into He who is love?

This is what God wants for you:

> [That you may really come] to know [practically, through experi-ence for yourselves] the love of Christ, **which far surpasses mere knowledge [without experience]; that you may be filled [through all your being]** unto all the fullness of God [may have the richest measure of the divine Presence, and become a body **wholly filled and flooded with God Himself**]!" (v. 19 AMPC)

Jesus doesn't want us to just know about Him; He wants us to experience His ever-increasing fullness inside our hearts. He wants ownership of our hearts.

This is how a heart goes from deceptive to receptive. Experience, surpassing mere knowledge, changes the thoughts of the heart, which changes the mind. Read that Scripture again: "The love of Christ, which far surpasses mere knowledge [without experience]" can fill us with "*the richest measure* of the divine Presence," so we "become a body *wholly filled and flooded* with God Himself."

I want to be wholly filled and flooded with God Himself. Then, just as an earth-crawling, dust-eating caterpillar transforms into a wonder-filled, busting-out, high-flying butterfly, I will become a wholly new creation. It's not that I wasn't a new creation before, because God says I was (2 Cor. 5:17), but now, more than profess-ing that truth, through experience I am now possessing it.

How We Never Go about Knowing and Transforming

"How does this happen?" I hear some of you asking. Before we get into that, let me first tell you how it doesn't happen.

I committed to not looking at the news when writing portions of this book. Why? Because I am what I consume. Remember, "As [we] thinketh in [our hearts], so [are we]" (Prov. 23:7 KJV). When I read the news, I thinketh the news.

But I guess you could say I was in a bored moment, between dishes and bedtime duty . . . and social media called my name. Frankly, I wanted to do something mindless, and I like learning. I needed a rest moment. So, sitting on my gray bedroom couch, I took the bait and started scrolling. I read a couple of news articles. And then some more. I got sucked in.

It wasn't long until I began to feel upset about what I read. And the next day, as my husband took me on a two-hour trip to a writing destination in the mountains, rather than praying about writing this book, I started talking about those news articles and about politics, my mind spinning theories about what was probably happening.

I was doing exactly what I didn't want to do. I wanted my mind and heart to be holy ground for Jesus to fill with His thoughts, but I couldn't keep my eyes on Jesus, and now I was blabbing, wandering off on divergent paths . . . and therein lies the problem.

Divided attention steals heart devotion to Jesus and side-steps the power of mind-transforming affection.

Many of us struggle with roaming eyes. We sit down to spend time with Jesus only to get to thinking about how we really need to buy that white sweater online before everyone else does. We put on music to connect to God in worship, but all of a sudden we remember we need to call our friend back from last week. We sit, prepared to connect deeply to the promptings of God's heart, and a fly comes buzzing past. We need to get the fly swatter. We pull ourselves out of intimacy.

Roaming-eye issues interrupt experiences of love about to happen.

Jesus said, "Martha, Martha, you are anxious and troubled about many things, but one thing is necessary. Mary has chosen the good portion, which will not be taken away from her" (Luke 10:41–42 ESV).

Sitting and beholding Jesus, like Mary did at His feet, is how we are transformed into His very image. We cannot afford to take our eyes off Jesus. Without experiencing Him, we will not receive the expanding and exploding fullness of Him in our hearts. We will get busy with many things. We will get scared when God starts to lead us into the depths of His love, and we'll shut down our welcome to God and shut a door in His face.

Would you want to be an abiding guest at a house in which you are unwelcome? Where someone shuts the door on you?

I can't help but feel that, for some of us, Jesus has been trying to knock on the door of our hearts. He wants in. He wants greater access. He wants to take us deeper, but our fascination with other things, our distractions with busyness, our affections regarding who we think we have to be, or our declarations and feelings about who we are not have shut down our attention to Jesus.

Jesus said to the Jewish leaders, "I have come in My Father's name and with His power, and you do not receive Me [*your hearts are not open to Me, you give Me no welcome*]" (John 5:43 AMPC). Let that not be said of us. There is no experience with Jesus if we shut the door in His face.

Let us never shut the door in Jesus's face, for then the power of *ginosko* knowing will never result in mind renewal through experience.

Knowing Is Growing

All four of us—my husband and our two kids and I—were driving high up in the Appalachian Mountains of North Carolina.

Careening through dense trees and coming up through high plateaus of rock, we had the ultimate goal of getting to a particular hiking trail, one that apparently had the best views in the area. The road was narrow. A sharp drop-off lay to our right side.

Without a moment's notice, in a second of distraction, my husband lost control of the car. He bumped onto the right side of the road—and jerked the wheel back to the left. The car almost went over the edge—but it didn't.

After regaining control, my husband yelled out, "Wow! Angels must have just protected us. We should have gone over the edge."

My ten-year-old, Michael, replied, "Dad? It's amazing to know God will protect me in everything. So, really, I don't have to fear anything."

My daughter, Madison, agreed too.

It was through an illuminating experience that my children arrived to this biblical revelation that brought mind renewal. While I love God's Word and regularly try to teach it to them, it didn't happen by me teaching and reading to them, "So do not fear, for I am with you; do not be dismayed, for I am your God. I will strengthen you and help you; I will uphold you with my righteous right hand" (Isa. 41:10). Experience ingrained this truth into my children's minds in a way my best lessons never could. They learned *I don't have to fear. God really is in charge.* Isaiah 41:10 became real truth.

Often we can open the door to experiencing God by noticing God. His sheep hear His voice. God's voice probably doesn't sound like God speaking from heaven to you with a microphone. He whispers in our hearts when we read the Word. He nudges us to call a friend. He pulls us toward Him with environmental reminders.

I wonder, What is the Shepherd saying to you? What is He revealing? Where is He leading you? What is He calling you into? What reminds you of Him? What Scripture does He want to turn into a feast for you, so much so that it lays claim to you inside and out, via the flooding of Jesus? How does He drop letters of love in your midst on a daily basis?

"Taste and see that the LORD is good; blessed is the one who takes refuge in him" (Ps. 34:8).

"In your presence there is fullness of joy; at your right hand are pleasures forevermore" (16:11 ESV).

"Because your love is better than life, my lips will glorify you" (63:3).

"A single day in your courts is better than a thousand anywhere else!" (84:10 NLT).

By beholding His love, we become it (and think it).

The same Mary who sat at Jesus's feet in Luke 10 later poured out liquid perfume as she beheld Him in John 12. When this happened, a fragrant aroma filled the room. Likewise, when we pour out love on Jesus, we smell like love. What we bathe in, we smell of. What we soak in soaks into us.

Where are you soaking your mind? What are you filling it up with? What do you smell like?

As Christ takes up more room in our hearts, as we see Him throughout our every day, and as we are pondering Him in our minds, the thoughts of His heart become the thoughts of ours. We no longer have to focus so much on conforming (or sin management) when our eyes are taken over by the wonder and power of His transforming work within us.

> What eye has not seen and ear has not heard and has not entered into the heart of man, [all that] God has prepared (made and keeps ready) for those who love Him [who hold Him in affectionate reverence, promptly obeying Him and gratefully recognizing the benefits He has bestowed]. (1 Cor. 2:9 AMPC)

Our minds cannot be left the same in the wake of experiencing God's love. When we are filled to overflowing by the power of the Holy Spirit, streams of living water flow everywhere, out of us.

Then, thinking like Christ, acting like Him, and feeling as He feels isn't hard labor; it is just *who we are*.

As we experientially know the mind of Christ and welcome it in our hearts, we release the fragrant aroma of Christ Himself. And everyone takes notice. Because our new love is completely inconsistent with who we used to be and how we used to love. Only God could do something like that and transform a person that way.

And we know the secret: it happened through *ginosko* experience. We don't just know about God; we know Him in the depths of our minds—we really know Him! And why bother thinking about lesser things?

DECLARATION

I am a person of devotion, wholly given over to God-centered affection. I give Him all my attention and am not thrown off by distractions.

Homework

- We see God in nature.
- We hear God in the words of a friend.
- We experience God in the wind that reminds us of His power.
- We encounter His heart through the Word that comes alive and speaks to us.
- We behold and become like Him as we worship Him in spirit and truth.
- We see something happen around us and know it is a message for us.
- We are aware that there is a message coming through, one we'd never recognize if we were too busy or distracted.
- We worship, we praise, and we thank God. We experience His comfort and leading.
- We hear the Shepherd's voice.

  The sheep that are My own hear and are listening to My voice; and I know them, and they follow Me. (John 10:27 AMPC)

Yesterday, I sensed God saying to me, *Kelly, I will do it.*

Unsure of what he was talking about, I prayed (asked back), "What, God? What will You do?"

I sat there, thinking He would help me write this book or love my husband more.

Then I felt a nudge in me. It was Him saying, *Everything.*

He will do everything—for me. That moved me. God wants to do everything for me, if I'll let Him. He cares that much.

I let this truth settle into me. I sat with it. I thought on it.

And peace flooded my heart. *God will do everything. In fact, He already has, on the cross.* He said, *"It is finished"* (19:30).

What is God saying to you in this hour?

Perceive and hear the mind of Christ.

———— Prayer ————

Father, I thank You for Jesus. I thank You that You want Him to be mine in greater measure. I want that. I long for Him. I live for Him. I ask You to keep me from distraction so that full devotion can take me over. I ask for heart attention when I feel afraid. I thank You that Jesus loves me so much. He proved this when He gave it all for me on the cross. I can trust Him. I can lean into Him. I can rely on Him. I can believe the words the Shepherd whispers. Give me faith. Faith is required in this walk to experience His profound love. Faith is a gift; I ask You for it. In Jesus's name. Amen.

———— Free Download ————

Download "25 Ways to Experience God Afresh" at www.itakethoughtscaptive.com.

6

Respond, Don't React

Focus on giants—you stumble. Focus on God—your giants tumble.

Max Lucado, *Cast of Characters*

You purchase a dream home. It's beautiful. It has gorgeous stonework lining the chimney and a palatial feel. It's ten thousand square feet of bliss. After spending $1.8 million, you are ready to settle down, kick up your feet, and enjoy life a little. The only thing is, you can't. You have a problem on your hands. A big one.

This is exactly what happened to a Maryland family whose dream house turned into a house of horrors.

Why? How?

Their new house had an infestation problem . . . specifically, snakes. Snakes took over their home, creeping and crawling everywhere. The prior owners had struggled with these same snakes in a similar way.

So much for a dream home. The owners must have been freaked out, wondering, *Will snakes creep and crawl on me at night? What happens if I leave my mouth open? Am I safe?*

This family, stressed by the sheer terror of it all, took things into their own hands. Trying to smoke out the snakes, they lit coal inside the house. They might have succeeded in smoking out the snakes—but instead they burned their $1.8 million house down to the ground. Their quick reaction caused a destructive fire.[1]

The lesson here: quick reactions cause destructive fires. They burn relationships.

Have you, in haste, damaged relationships due to quick reactions?

If you have, you're not alone. I've been there too.

Reacting Lights Fires

In the morning, I get all caught up in God's Word and how it is coming alive. I sit on my front porch with the scent of beautiful flowers surrounding me. I marvel at what God is showing me, and I think deeply about it. I love my time with God. A sense of peace and calm settles on me. I know, then, as I consider my day: *God's got this.*

I breathe deep; I can be still and know that He is God.

Yet, at lunch, say my husband comes in the door and tells me he has a plan for our family to move. Suddenly I lose it. His plan is radically different from mine, and it feels like a big problem— and one I will have to pack up. God seems to have gone missing, and I am panicked. I lose my peace. I lose my connection to love. I start hindering God's welcome. Why? Because I am stressed out and burdened.

I no longer can "be still, and know that [He is] God" (Ps. 46:10). Rather than waiting patiently on the Lord, to be led forward by the mind of Christ, by the thoughts of Christ, sourced from the heart of Christ—I react.

"I don't want to move!" I tell him.

And all peace goes. An argument may ensue. I move from being a welcoming, open door for Christ to a fear-ball, a raging, reactive fire of emotions.

I'm no longer anywhere near this place:

> One thing I have asked from the LORD, that I shall seek:
> That I may dwell in the house of the LORD all the days of my life,
> To behold the beauty of the LORD
> And to meditate in His temple. (27:4 NASB)

There is no beauty to see now, only a fire set by my quick reaction. And I panic, because now I have to figure out how to put it out.

What triggers you to react? Is it when you feel misunderstood? Misheard? Disregarded? Ignored? Rejected? Confronted?

Keeping Connection

> Dwell in Me, and I will dwell in you. [Live in Me, and I will live in you.] Just as no branch can bear fruit of itself without abiding in (being vitally united to) the vine, neither can you bear fruit unless you abide in Me.
>
> I am the Vine; you are the branches. Whoever lives in Me and I in him bears much (abundant) fruit. However, **apart from Me [cut off from vital union with Me] you can do nothing.**
>
> If a person does not dwell in Me, he is thrown out like a [broken-off] branch, and withers; such branches are gathered up and thrown into the fire, and they are burned.
>
> If you live in Me [abide vitally united to Me] and My words remain in you **and continue to live in your hearts**, ask whatever you will, and it shall be done for you. (John 15:4–7 AMPC)

Without connection to Christ we should not expect to see real fruit. Apart from Christ we can do nothing. In this state we are cut off. Our prayer line to God is down. Without dwelling in Him we are out of alignment and will miss God-assignments. Only via connection is there great reception to our prayers.

How many of us are not seeing answered prayers because, rather than being filled with the Spirit, we are living by the flesh and reacting with anger, fear, irritation, worry, or a sense of being overwhelmed?

It is not what happens that dictates our lives; it is how we respond to it. Do we respond united to Christ's heart (what He has said, what fruits He is leading us to release, what hope He brings), or do we act on impulse?

Jesus said, "I have loved you, [just] as the Father has loved Me; abide in My love [continue in His love with Me]" (v. 9 AMPC). When we abide in Jesus's love, we spread it far and wide.

"When you bear (produce) much fruit, My Father is honored and glorified, and you show and prove yourselves to be true followers of Mine" (v. 8 AMPC).

If people know us by our fruit, it is fruit that shines Jesus out of us. I should know; I've tried to tell people about Jesus ad nauseum, but nothing speaks louder than a simple four-letter word: *love*. Especially when it is sacrificial love, moving out in action.

What does all this mean?

It means that if we want to stay connected to the mind of Christ, we must, at all costs—no matter what force is coming against us, no matter how violent a person's words or how horribly our house has been burned to the ground—choose to

Stay calm in order to pray and decipher the Lord's encouragement and path.

Remain at peace to reach people with Him who is the Prince of Peace.

Remain in His love by pondering His Word, feeling His love, and receiving the truth in our hearts even more than in our minds.

84

Hear His heart by being still and by listening (John 10:27).

Step away, do something else, and give ourselves space before speaking mean words or making the wrong decision.

Think upon Jesus's grace, love, power, and ability to help us in all things, in all ways, and at all times.

Without doing these things, we drop our connectivity with God. And when we drop our connection, we also lose our union with the indwelling Holy Spirit. This is a sad state of affairs. The Holy Spirit, the Spirit of Christ (Phil. 1:19), is trying to lead us in all things, at all times, in all ways, in all reactions, in all words, and in all actions by the very mind of Christ.

No matter the onslaught, the distraction, the problem, the person—do not allow yourself to be cut off from the Vine.

How to Respond versus React

My friend Marcia is an amazing teacher. She goes all out to love first graders and do activities with them. She just pours and pours out love. I am sure she often works up a good hunger after a full day of chasing kids around.

One day, after a busy time at work and a whole bunch of activities, Marcia needed to eat. It was 3:00 p.m. She was hungry!

So she whipped herself up some leftover Thanksgiving stuffing and gravy and made a soup concoction—a whole pot of yum. And then she ate. Apparently, about halfway through the pot, her stomach registered as full. She was done—or was she? Marcia told me that right about this point, when she was deciding whether to keep eating or not, the Holy Spirit caused her to pause and consider what her body was telling her.

Yet she ignored the nudge. She kept right on eating until the pot was empty and her belly was stuffed full.

And not much later, she suffered the consequences. She was tired, groggy, and miserable, and she felt cruddy for the rest of the day.

Marcia had welcomed in disconnection rather than heeding wisdom. As a result, she lacked peace and found herself in a state of dissonance. Rather than responding to her body's signals, she'd continued doing her own thing, her own way—reacting to a pot of yum.

Jesus said to the Jews,

> And you have not **His word** (**His thought**) living in your hearts, because you do not believe and adhere to and trust in and rely on Him Whom He has sent. [That is why you do not keep His message living in you, because you do not believe in the Messenger Whom He has sent.] (John 5:38 AMPC)

Many times, like Marcia did, we react to what tastes good in the moment instead of responding. We don't trust the mind of Christ. We don't think His way is our best way, or as good as our own way. We don't think the nudge is really God. We don't think God cares that much if we obey or disobey. We don't trust God to defend us. We don't want to rely on anyone but ourselves. We don't feel like waiting on God when we can do something faster. We don't think something we can't understand could possibly be the right way to go. We don't think that other person will change without our two cents. We don't trust prayer.

Lack of trust leads us to doubt everything in our minds. Or to react emotionally. But we don't have to react to the stimuli of life. We can choose to respond only to Christ.

How do we do this? To respond rather than react, we use the four Rs. These four Rs are preemptive. Consider them a filter. They stop thoughts before they get into our minds. They elaborate and clarify some of the points we've already covered in this chapter to make them easier for us to remember day to day. If we start with them, we likely won't need all the other steps of the process to take every thought captive that we'll talk about in part 3.

These four *R*s are an escape route, before the thought enters your mind, so you don't get set on fire with emotion. If you divert an altercation, you won't have to walk out such lengthy mind-remediation. The goal with these 4 Rs is to stop the problem before it happens. The more you practice, the more you train your mind in self-control.

Here are the four *R*s, designed to help us preemptively respond versus emotionally react:

1. *Remind.* We remind ourselves that we do not have to react immediately. This means we can tell our emotions to sit down for a second. We don't need to have answers right away. Instant solutions are not required. Getting alone with God is. The only thing we *need* to do is stay connected to peace and rely on His love to carry us through.

2. *Remember.* "We have the mind of Christ (the Messiah) and do hold the thoughts (feelings and purposes) of His heart" (1 Cor. 2:16 AMPC) in our hearts. In this, we pause to discern and understand what God would have us to do (Eph. 5:10) and what God has to say to us as individuals. We identify what feelings and purposes of His heart He is trying to convey. We consider the Word of God, which is the very thoughts of God, and prepare to put it into practice. We stay in His love, even if the world tries to push us out of it. We also evaluate if we are reacting based on the past or even how we were treated as a child. Sometimes unhealed childhood pain can cause strong emotional triggers. There are times when what is coming at us is not even that bad; it is just interpreted as an offense due to past pain. This is where we have to be really honest with ourselves.

3. *Respond.* Simply, we obey Him. "Jesus replied, 'Anyone who loves me will obey my teaching'" (John 14:23). To obey may mean we do the opposite of what our first

reaction was. If it is hard to do this, be encouraged: It is hard to die to our flesh. It is hard to do things a new way. It is hard to love others in the face of what first felt horrible.

4. *Rest*. Rest is keeping our minds stayed on God. In this, we thank Him. We thank Him for leading us in the way to go. We thank Him that the mind of Christ teaches us the very thoughts of God. We thank Him for His Word. We worship. We do whatever we need to do to stay our minds on Jesus and to keep in a place of trust. "You will keep in perfect peace those whose minds are steadfast, because they trust in you" (Isa. 26:3).

We can rest because Jesus always has our victory. "In all these things we are more than conquerors through him who loved us" (Rom. 8:37).

The goal in responding is to stay connected to the Spirit of God. To live united versus divided from Him. To remain vitally linked to the very mind of Christ. Only then can we—in partnership with the conviction, consolation, and direction of the Holy Spirit—effectively take every thought captive. By doing this, we sidestep our fear of failure, demise, embarrassment, shame, or humiliation, or our people-pleasing tendencies.

Connection is soul harmony and solidarity.

And let the peace (soul harmony which comes) from Christ rule (act as umpire continually) in your hearts [deciding and settling with finality all questions that arise in your minds, in that peaceful state] to which as [members of Christ's] one body you were also called [to live]. (Col. 3:15 AMPC)

Where Responding Leads Us

Once we begin to use the four *R*s, due to our ever-growing connection with God, more light bulbs turn on. We gain understanding.

A man of understanding and wisdom **has a cool spirit (self-control, an even temper)**. (Prov. 17:27 AMP)

Paul wrote,

I pray that your hearts will be flooded with light so that you can understand **the confident hope** he has given to those he called—his holy people who are his rich and glorious inheritance.

I also pray that you will **understand the incredible greatness of God's power for us who believe him.** This is the same mighty power that raised Christ from the dead and seated him in the place of honor at God's right hand in the heavenly realms. (Eph. 1:18–20 NLT)

In the gap of not reacting, we gain understanding. The word *understanding* is defined by Merriam-Webster as "an agreement of opinion or feeling: adjustment of differences."[2] It has its origins in the biblical Greek word *dianoia*, which means understanding in mind or imagination.[3] Understanding is where God goes about making divine mental adjustments on us.

Understanding is the next level of knowing. It is a higher level of receiving. It is agreeing readily with Christ—His power, His being, His feelings. It is the culmination point of transformation. Responding (instead of reacting) helps us to go about understanding. It gives white space for God to move, speak, and reveal His truth to us.

Then, we *ginosko* know and think thoughts like, *What can stop me when God is for me?* We see things afresh. Our problem gets small and His help gets big. Our original interpretation becomes shallow water; His leading takes us into the depths. This happens when we remain in Christ, thinking as He thinks, overflowing with His love, and rising above our issues.

Here, we look different from everyone else. Christ in us, the hope of all glory, shines! Our relationship with God rises to a new level. It is where soul harmony and solidarity become ours. And it is an encouraging place to be, because we know that we are—more and more—becoming and thinking like Him.

DECLARATION

"In all these things we are more than conquerors through him who loved us" (Rom. 8:37).

Homework

Think of a time when God gave you understanding of an issue. What did your understanding do in your heart? How did it change how you saw things? How did He deliver that understanding to you? What were you able to learn? Thank God for this understanding. Then ask God to increase your understanding, discernment, and wisdom. Ask Him to help you respond versus react so you can always stay connected to His heart.

Prayer

Father, I do not want to be emotionally reactive. I do not want to blow up when things go wrong. I want to stay in Your love and keep Your peace. Give me the grace to remain in You. To abide in Your love. You are greater than my life. You are the fullness of joy. All my fountains are in You. I want You more than life itself. Jesus, thank You for saving me. Save me again. In Jesus's name. Amen.

Free Download

Download "10 Practical Tips to be Patient" and "How to Respond Calmly" at www.itakethoughtscaptive.com.

7

Say, "Shut Up, Devil!"

So when the devil throws your sins in your face and declares that you deserve death and hell, tell him this: "I admit that I deserve death and hell, what of it? For I know One who suffered and made satisfaction on my behalf. His name is Jesus Christ, Son of God, and where He is there I shall be also!"

Martin Luther, *Letters of Spiritual Counsel*

I drove by an indistinguishable pile of red, raw meat torn up on the side of the road. Roadkill. Whatever that animal *was*, it *was not* anything like that anymore. I didn't want to look at it, and a thought occurred to me: *The devil wants to rip you apart like that, Kelly. Without God defending you, that's what you'd look like.*

The devil only hopes our minds can be his playground. Our "adversary the devil prowls around like a roaring lion, seeking someone to devour" (1 Pet. 5:8 ESV).

The devil hasn't come to play patty-cake with us; he has come to destroy and devour us. His battleground is our minds.

Killer of God's Seed

Frankly, while I wrote this book, there were some major attacks. Not only did I struggle with not being able to walk for weeks without crutches but everything was combusting around me. For instance, I kept getting annoyed and irritated at my husband and kids, about dumb things—for no good reason.

In each evening following each horrible day, I'd recount how badly I'd acted. In my head I would hear, *Who are you, Kelly, to write this book?* I actually considered letting the publisher know I could not write this book anymore. I was so angry at myself.

Relentlessly, I heard, *You are the biggest hypocrite ever. What right do you have to write a book about something you haven't conquered? What do you have to teach anyone? Are you even taking your thoughts captive?*

Those days, I feared being a hypocrite (and I still am not perfect, by the way).

But I realized to submit to the devil would be to sidestep Jesus's grace. God's work is not dependent on my work; it is dependent on His. I would not fall into the devil's setup and schemes (Eph. 6:11).

Eventually I came to this conclusion: *Who cares what the enemy is doing when Christ has already won my freedom? Who cares what condemnation he is telling me when it is God's power at work in this book and not mine? His grace is enough! And it is enough to help me be kind to my family too.*

It's not about me.

"I have been crucified with Christ and I no longer live, but Christ lives in me" (Gal. 2:20). After repentance, there's no *me*. There's Jesus and what He is doing, the grace He gives. I am free when I see myself as a new creation (holy, pure, forgiven, in Christ), no matter what stone-throwing the enemy tries.

Beyond this, God's "divine power has given us everything we need for a godly life through our knowledge of him who called us by his own glory and goodness" (2 Pet. 1:3). The knowledge of the Father, Son, and Holy Spirit is all I need!

And so, in that time, I prayed and sought God, and then I realized I might have a hormone imbalance. I added a vitamin, and I started acting like a different person. God has all we need to defeat the enemy—every time, in every way—without us resorting to condemnation. Instead of being angry and irritable, I could abide with God and love my family.

We force the devil to shake in his boots when we stand in Christ and the power of Jesus that overcomes! Knowing His victory is knowing things may kill our flesh but cannot kill our soul (Matt. 10:28). The power of Christ cannot be broken!

God always has been and always will be victorious (Ps. 110:5–7).

Forbid the Devil to Shame-Game You

Just yesterday, my son and I laid out everything for his school Christmas pop-up market. Our table looked sparkling and brilliant. Beautiful greens, gorgeous reds, and luxurious golds shined out of our wreaths, candles, and ornaments. It was seriously picture-perfect. I snapped some photos and posed with my son. Huge smiles! Even though we didn't say it, I'm pretty sure both of us thought, *We have this. We're going to nail this event!*

I figured he'd walk away with far more money than we'd spent on supplies, and I would be a great momma who helped him win. My hope was he'd forget everything leading up to this moment— how our glitter bombs had busted everywhere and how, at times, I'd been stressed. I felt so bad about that. So guilty. I confessed but still felt oppressed in my heart.

I wanted to gloss over all that had previously happened, mainly the fact that I'm not perfect. *Cover, Kelly! Make up for your lack, Kelly. Be flawless, Kelly. Show him you are worthy of love, Kelly.*

This day had to be a big win.

People came, and my son and I put on our biggest and brightest smiles. We sold stuff. Yet our hot-ticket item, our wreaths, just weren't selling. Those things were as beautiful as lemon meringue on a warm summer day—yet people passed them by. So, at the end of the day, after we counted the money, we had not made a profit.

My son started crying. I got tense and afraid. *Fix it, Kelly. Fix it.* How could I save the day?

I tried to calm him, but he kept crying.

Then, in a momentary lapse of good judgment plus a good dose of fear, I freaked out. I saw him rubbing his teary face with his germ-laden, cash-touching hands (during the coronavirus pandemic), and all I could say was, "Go wash your hands. You don't want to get sick."

You jerk, Kelly! What are you doing? What is wrong with you?!

Then I tried to fix everything, including every single one of his feelings, by saying, "I'll buy everything left for half price."

Because Kelly Balarie is the savior of shame! His and also my own.

I wonder, Have you ever felt hit by shame? Is self-hatred or condemnation hard to shake after you already confessed it to God?

Maybe you think, *It's embarrassing to feel weak. I'm not good enough. God has to be tired of all my mistakes. I can't do things right.* How do you deal with shame? With being charged in your mind? Or, I guess the better question to ask is, How did Jesus deal with it?

> He canceled the record of the charges against us and took it away by nailing it to the cross. In this way, **he disarmed the spiritual rulers** and authorities. **He shamed them publicly** by his victory over them on the cross. (Col. 2:14–15 NLT)

Jesus made a public spectacle of shame, throwing the mud of His victory in the devil's face. The light of His grace now floods out the darkness of the shame trying to darken and dampen our views. Jesus took all our shame to the cross so it doesn't have to stay on us.

Five Breakthrough Tips When Shame Comes In like a Flood

So you may be wondering, what happened with me and my son? And how did I overcome? I used five key tactics that brought my breakthrough; these tips may help you too.

One: Bring Shame to the Light

With my son, I said something like, "Son, I didn't do a good job when I reacted in fear. I rushed in to make things better for you. It is okay for you to have your feelings. I'm sorry I wasn't more loving and sensitive. I forgive me, and Jesus forgives me too."

And then I internally repented and let the whole bad scenario die like an unwanted bug. All the while, I reminded myself that it was okay for my son to feel sad. We all have feelings. He could have his feelings and I—while listening to God's voice—could walk through mine.

Two: Remind Yourself of What Jesus Said

In the middle of the night, I woke up thinking about my son, and the enemy started back up in my mind. I reminded myself, *It is finished. God says He remembers my sin no more.* These truths make the enemy scram!

I am not my sin. I am not a sacrificial lamb; only Jesus was. After repentance, the act of God forgiving me is done. To receive all this, I often declare truths such as:

Who the son sets free is free indeed (John 8:36).
I am righteous, holy, and pure in the eyes of Christ (Eph. 1:4).
I am beloved. I am forgiven. There is so much grace for me
(2 Cor. 12:9).

95

Three: Renounce Lies and Receive Truth

It wasn't true that I was messing up my child. Instead of believing this lie, I received the truth that the grace of Jesus was more than enough to cover my mistakes.

Four: Find What Is Good

I reminded myself that I was learning, and when we are learning, we are not failing. We are growing so we can react in new ways in the future.

Five: Look to Jesus

I kept my mind on the way He overcame. I remembered to look "unto Jesus the author and finisher of our faith; who for the joy that was set before him endured the cross, *despising the shame*, and is set down at the right hand of the throne of God" (Heb. 12:2 KJV).

If Jesus despised the shame for the greater gain, so can we. According to Strong's Concordance, the Greek word translated "despising" here is *kataphroneō*, which means to "think little or nothing of."[1] When shame comes knocking again, we can think nothing of it!

Handling Other Attacks

Do you know what a stronghold is?

> For the weapons of our warfare are not physical [weapons of flesh and blood], but they are mighty before God **for the overthrow and destruction of strongholds**, [inasmuch as we] **refute arguments** and **theories** and **reasonings** and **every proud and lofty thing** that sets itself up against the [true] knowledge of God; and we lead every thought and purpose away captive into the obedience of Christ (the Messiah, the Anointed One). (2 Cor. 10:4–5 AMPC)

In ancient days, a stronghold was an impenetrable fortress that protected a city. It was the maker or breaker of life in a town or city. To lose the fortress was to lose the life and safety of the city.

Strongholds within our minds happen the same way. If we strongly hold God, our godly stronghold will bring life to us. But if the enemy gets a stronghold in our minds, he will take territory with his lies.

How does the enemy gain a hold in our minds? Through reasonings, arguments, theories, and lofty things, he continues to repeat lie after lie. Tell a lie long enough, and a person starts to believe it. They let go of old beliefs and form new neural pathways and experiences that send their beliefs a new way.

This is why we have to hold firmly and strongly to godly beliefs, lest new mental holds form. Demonic strongholds should have no place in our minds.

This is why the work we have been doing to place our hearts in the right posture is so vital. Wholehearted people relying on God's truths become far less penetrable to demonic arrows. We prevent strongholds from forming by keeping near truth and a true knowledge of God.

For instance, during hard times, we may need to remember our lives are "now hidden with Christ in God" (Col. 3:3). We may recite, "The LORD [is] invincible in battle" (Ps. 24:8 NLT). We dwell on these sorts of things.

When I do so, I can't help but think, *If I am in Christ and Christ is invincible in battle, how can the enemy ever find me?* I have a godly argument instead of a demonic one that consistently insists, *Ah! I'm about to die!* Mental attacks can't find me.

We fight strongholds in our minds by returning to true knowledge of our position in Christ Jesus. The devil cannot take Jesus down.

Jesus told us, "Remain in me, as I also remain in you" (John 15:4). When we remember we are in Christ, and Christ is in us, we move back into untouchable status. This is how we live out this verse: "Don't let your hearts be troubled. Trust in God, and trust also in me" (14:1 NLT).

Can we trust God? Of course we can. Sometimes we have to tell our mind what to do. Sometimes we have to say, *Mind, you can trust God and you will. It will start now!* Then we let go of all other theories, arguments, and reasoning and all the things we've been plagued by.

When I don't know what is up and what is down—when my thought life gets ultra-confusing, and the enemy is trying to shake my heart—I encourage myself. I cheerlead my soul. I say things like:

> God is going to teach me about being a good wife and a good mom.
>
> God is going to carry me out the other side and make me stronger.
>
> God is going to show up and lead me in the way I should go.

"And we know that God works all things together for the good of those who love Him, who are called according to His purpose" (Rom. 8:28 BSB). There is no trial that God will not make into triumph through Christ. I don't care how difficult the journey is.

This is how you can tell the devil to shut up. This is how you wield the sword of the Spirit. You recite His truth. You remain hidden in Christ. You remember His power and might.

God's sheep hear His voice (John 10:27). Align your mind to His. A posture like this strangles the enemy's voice once and for all!

DECLARATION

I am not what I feel. I am not what happens to me. I am a beloved daughter, and nothing can separate me from the love of God. I can boldly approach Jesus's throne.

———— Homework ————

Hebrews 4:15–16 is truth to stand on:

> For we do not have a High Priest Who is unable to understand and sympathize and have a shared feeling with our weaknesses and infirmities and liability to the assaults of temptation, but One Who has been tempted in every respect as we are, yet without sinning.
>
> Let us then fearlessly and confidently and boldly draw near to the throne of grace (the throne of God's unmerited favor to us sinners), that we may receive mercy [for our failures] and find grace to help in good time for every need [appropriate help and well-timed help, coming just when we need it]. (AMPC)

Your homework is to:

1. Seek to understand how your High Priest understands, sympathizes, *and* has a shared feeling with your weaknesses, infirmities, and liabilities to the assaults of temptation. The knowledge that God understands our struggles can mean so much!

2. Recognize all that Jesus went through and how He stood through trial. Praise Him and thank Him for it. Use your mouth to do so, not only your mind.

3. Boldly go before God for every single need you have. Ask Him for help in taking down strongholds. Confess to Him. Request His assistance. Need Him.

4. Receive mercy, love, and help from Him, by faith, in this process. Write down what this looks like.

———— Prayer ————

Father God, I ask You to keep me from evil and temptation. I ask that I would be strong in hope, steady in truth, and equipped with Your Word. May I remember all I have in Christ Jesus. I want to carry peace and be armed with faith. I ask that

I would not fall to the schemes or devices of the enemy but would stand strong through thought and action. May I be an overcomer in all my ways. Jesus, You triumph, always. I trust You to lead me and guide me in Your triumph. You are King of Kings and Lord of Lords. I love You, and I submit my thoughts and life to You today. In Jesus's name. Amen.

8

Avoid This Mentality at All Costs

Do you know that nothing you do in this life will ever matter,
unless it is about loving God and loving the people he has made?

Francis Chan, *Crazy Love*

Nearly every office seems to have *that* person. You know,
the one with whom encounters go something like this:

Me: "Where do I find the office supplies?"

Her: "You know where. The office closet." (looking at
me like I have horns on my head while slightly rolling her eyes and showing complete disdain on her
face)

Me: "And where is that?" (politely)

Her: "*They* didn't tell you?" (staring at me as if I am the
dumbest human on earth)

Me: "No. They didn't."

Whoever *they* were, *they* apparently were in the wrong, and now *they* had done it again, or so this woman thought. She thrust back her chair, sighed, and got up to show me the closet.

Hardly looking back at me, the lady grunted, "Follow me."

This was my first job, far off in the land of California. I'd made the big trip from Maryland just for this job. I certainly wasn't perfect. But still, couldn't the lady help me?

As time passed, I felt bad for her. She was always talking about why she should get a promotion. I knew she never would. Right after cataloging all the good things she did, inevitably she'd launch into a long monologue about the 101 ways everyone had crossed her and wronged her, and who the bad people were in the office.

If I had my wits about me, I'd excuse myself and run away before she got to this point.

The saddest part, though, was I'm pretty sure she knew inside that she'd never get that promotion. She'd remain at exactly the same place. Doing exactly the same thing. Because of that one thing she insisted on carrying within her, the one thing that ruined everything: bitterness.

This woman had a major bitter root. Bitterness often blocks blessing. It also kills joy and corrupts hearts. "Each heart knows its own bitterness, and no one else can share its joy" (Prov. 14:10). And it is one of the things that "above all else" we must guard our hearts from receiving.

> Look after each other so that none of you fails to receive the grace of God. Watch out **that no poisonous root of bitterness** grows up to **trouble you, corrupting many.** (Heb. 12:15 NLT)

To *corrupt* means to "rot, spoil" or "to alter from the original or correct form or version."[1] Bitterness doesn't spoil the ones who hurt us. Note: it spoils us. Might we have a bitter root?

Do we hate people who have things better than us?

102

Do we hold back from praying for blessings for others?
Do we covet things and harbor resentment about what we
   didn't get?
Do we feel ripped off?
Do we have a hard time praying for certain people?
Do we put people down in our minds?

Our root-life determines our fruit-life. A bitter root will create bad fruit. We can't go around with a bitter root and expect to walk in joy and life. Bad roots do not make good fruit. Nor do they make good disciples of Jesus that shine His light to unbelievers. "For each tree is known by its own fruit" (Luke 6:44 ESV).

The only way to handle a bitter root is to yank out the whole underground root system. It can be a lot to pull out at one time (I should know). But the entire root must be plucked up— accompanying thoughts and all.

That woman I worked with probably thought, *People here are against me. Leadership doesn't appreciate me. I do everything and get nothing back. People don't value or see me. I hate this place. No one likes me.*

Entitlement is a major source of bitter roots: *I deserve this. I should have this. I should be treated better. Things are unfair. No one appreciates me.*

Negative and condemning thoughts can point to bitter roots. Edgy, sour, and/or walled-up behaviors can be resultant bad fruit from bad thoughts.

I've observed that before long, bitter people start to get eyebrows that furrow in, their smile disappears, and they become defensive, abrasive, condemning, and retaliatory. You can't talk to them for five minutes without an annoyance or perturbance coming out, even if you were talking about something entirely different. No one wants to be around someone like that.

Think of a root system under a tree. Bitter roots take up a lot of mental space when we let them grow. They directly impact the results of our lives. To think as Christ thinks, to love as He loves, and to act as He acts, we cannot act from roots of bitterness. Some warning signs that we are doing so include:

- Complaining, sighing, and constantly being annoyed.
- Thinking that life is unfair, we've been treated poorly, no one has done us right, or we deserve more.
- Coveting.
- Continually being upset and angry.
- Holding grudges and blaming people.
- Lacking appreciation.
- Being unable to celebrate others.
- Gossiping and backbiting.
- Sharing stories that subtly dog others or plant seeds of malice.
- Harboring unforgiveness or an unwillingness to forget.

Is this you?

What's the Big Deal? Bitterness Leads to Barrenness

The woman was spying on her husband.

> But as the Ark of the LORD entered the City of David, Michal, the daughter of Saul, looked down from her window. When she saw King David **leaping and dancing** before the LORD, **she was filled with contempt for him.** (2 Sam. 6:16 NLT)

What in the world is David doing now? she thought. *How dare he? He's dancing all crazy, like a wild man! He is a king, not a showman. That man is a show-off and a one-upper. My dad, King Saul, warned me about him. I should have listened. Look at David now. What makes him so free and happy anyway? He's clearly not thinking about me at all.*

104

Oh, I'll let him know how I feel about it.

When David returned home to bless his own family, his wife Michal, the daughter of Saul, came out to meet him. She said in disgust, "How distinguished the king of Israel looked today, *shamelessly exposing himself to the servant girls* like any vulgar person might do!" (v. 20 NLT).

Michal was furious. But what was David's perspective? Was he doing this to show off or to have women look at him? Or was he truly honoring God?

Let's look at what happened before David got home. His plan had been to carry the ark of the Lord to Jerusalem, but he didn't, mostly for reasons having to do with fear. So, for a time Obed-Edom had the ark, and Obed-Edom had received many blessings by doing so. Yet now David was busting through fear and getting the ark back. This was super exciting! He was joy-filled because he was moving forward. So much so that even before arriving home, he had been dancing "with shouts of joy and the blowing of rams' horns" (v. 15 NLT).

> David retorted to Michal, "I was dancing before the LORD, **who chose me** above your father and all his family! He appointed me as the leader of Israel, the people of the LORD, so I celebrate before the LORD. Yes, and **I am willing to look even more foolish** than this, **even to be humiliated in my own eyes!** But those servant girls you mentioned will indeed think I am distinguished!" (vv. 21–22 NLT)

This was a breakthrough moment for David.

But then there was Michal, who met him practically at the stoop of his front door, all ready to unleash.

Michal: "How dare you? You're so full of yourself!"
David: "Huh?"
Michal: "You are disgusting, exposing yourself to women!"

You can almost see Michal's squinty eyes, can't you? You can almost hear the internal dialogue she's having with herself. *He is so full of himself. He wants all those servant girls more than me. He has forgotten me. He is thinking of them. They love to watch him worship; they are in awe of him. He has so much joy. I have none. Why would he want me anyway?*

Bitterness fuels anger. It can make you hate who God created someone else to be.

Generationally, for Michal, the apple didn't fall far from the tree. The sin of the father was now the daughter's issue. Do you remember reading this in the Word?

> The women came out from all the towns of Israel to meet King Saul with singing and dancing, with joyful songs, and with timbrels and lyres. As they danced, they sang:
>
> "Saul has slain his thousands,
> and David his tens of thousands." (1 Sam. 18:6–7)

After this, Saul was so jealous that he put a death warrant on David's head. I can't imagine the bitterness about David that Michal may have overheard from her father. We must beware of listening to bitter stories. Make no mistake: listening to others' bitter stories can form bitter roots in us.

Don't allow someone else's gripe to become yours. Shut it down. Walk away. Do anything but allow their bitter sob story to enter your heart and poison your perspective, lest you become like Michal and aim to kill another person's joy because you decide you're being treated unfairly. Bitterness makes you beholden to old trauma.

Instead, mentally focus on what is good about the person before you. Maybe God has a plan for you two together, maybe there is something you can learn from them, maybe God wants to teach you something, or perhaps what they are doing is something you are also called to. Then bless the person.

There have been times in my life where a person I didn't like became my friend. On another occasion, when I got jealous of a friend's move, I felt angry at her! Well, once I got over my bitterness, I was freed up to realize that I wanted to move too. Then I moved to another state, and I was happy.

Real revelation hides behind delusional bitterness. To remove bitterness is to see truth.

I've found it is easy to resent someone else's freedom, especially if you've never tasted it. Resentment can happen. *They have what I only wish I could have.*

A wise thing to do is to ask yourself, *What is really going on inside my heart?* Remember, our hearts can lie, so look at the fruit and think of the thoughts that go with your relationships.

For instance, are you gossiping because of a person or because doing so makes you feel better than them? Are you competitive because that's how God made you or because you really don't feel like you are enough and you have to prove your worth?

What is really going on inside your mind? These are the sorts of things we want to be honest about. And repent of.

I know I've been guilty of ripping other people down because I felt bad about myself. Because I needed more attention. Because my thoughts were so focused on me, not on God. Whenever this happens, when bitterness sets in, I lose connection to the mind of Christ and operate self-absorbingly, only thinking about number-one Kelly.

Self-centeredness does not think God-centered thoughts.

I think this is what happened with Michal too—she became bitterly self-focused. And what happened as a result? "So Michal, the daughter of Saul, *remained childless* throughout her entire life" (2 Sam. 6:23 NLT).

Is this a coincidence? I don't think so. Bitterness breeds barrenness. Bitterness can't be blessed. Who wants to see *bitterness* reproduced and multiplied? Our world doesn't need more anger, hatred, fear, or retaliation—we all know that.

Banishing Bitterness

Ask my kids; I tell them all the time, "Attitude is everything." In his book *Happiness Is a Serious Problem*, Dennis Prager said,

> Yes, there is a "secret to happiness"—and it is gratitude. All happy people are grateful, and ungrateful people *cannot* be happy. We tend to think that it is being unhappy that leads people to complain, but it is truer to say that it is complaining that leads to people becoming unhappy.[2]

That's a thought, isn't it? It isn't what happens to us that predicts happiness but what we do with it. Attitude is everything.

I also go on to tell my kids, "If you arrive to your first day of work and complain about everything, what do you think will happen to you? Your first day of work will likely become your last day of work—and how will you feel then?"

To really overkill the point, then I say, "Think of this another way: if you are given ten gifts and don't say thank you, and leave the gifts outside to get rained on. The gift giver may think twice about giving you another gift in the future. That's just common sense."

Kids who think something is owed to them make for lousy gift recipients. It's easy to say, "Why bother giving them anything?!"

"Give me an attitude I can bless," I tell my kids. I say this because character-changing discipline needs to come if I don't see this. More important than any gift is their heart. Their attitude.

How do we have an attitude that God can bless? Where do we start? We start with forgiveness and release. "But if you do not forgive others their sins, your Father will not forgive your sins" (Matt. 6:15).

Forgiveness immediately removes the stronghold of bitterness.

One Thing That Destroys Bitter Entitlement

But there is one other thing we can do too. What else destroys entitled attitudes? What is a major antidote to bitterness? *Thankfulness.*

Thankfulness leads us into the healing presence of God.

> Enter into His gates with thanksgiving,
> And into His courts with praise.
> Be thankful to Him, and bless His name.
> For the LORD is good;
> His mercy is everlasting,
> And His truth endures to all generations. (Ps. 100:4–5 NKJV)

While bitter roots thrive in dry and parched ground where we figure "God never shows up," thankfulness recounts the goodness of God and rejoices in the splendor of all He's about to do.

Do you remember the ten lepers who went to Jesus for healing (Luke 17:11–19)? Nine didn't come back and say thank you. One did. That one got a deeper healing.

Gratitude heals deeply. What bitterness may you need to repent of, and what gratefulness can take its place?

Perhaps you are bitter that your husband always watches TV before hanging out with you at night. Maybe you can give thanks for what he does do and consider how he always prioritizes your Saturday date night. Maybe you can't stop obsessing about how a church leader hurt your feelings. Perhaps you forgive them and thank God that He is more than powerful enough to handle teaching that church leader whatever they need to know or learn.

If bitterness pops up, root it out like the warrior you are. Then give thanks; God has a better plan for you. Thanksgiving builds hope. Go and hope again!

Hope as you believe the best in others.

Hope as you trust God has a good plan.

Hope as you rely on God to handle the other person's problems with them.

It is written in Scripture that there are three things that last: faith, hope, and love (1 Cor. 13:13). When you operate with these three front and center in your mind instead of anger, bitterness, and judgment, you build into what is eternal instead of temporal. And, even more, you think like Christ, who is always full of faith, hope, and love.

Let these three things be the foundation of your mind, and you will have a good mind to love others well, influence them with hope, and offer them faith for impossible situations. You won't just find your mind renewed but filled with walk-on-water faith too.

DECLARATION

Love covers a multitude of sins. I choose to root myself in faith, hope, and love—like Jesus did—instead of anger, bitterness, and judgment.

Homework

I am led to share a story here that I really don't feel like sharing . . . but I will.

I couldn't forgive my father for a long time. I feel bad admitting this. I dragged everything he'd done around with me—pulling all his old little offenses around like dead fish strung on a line. Because I carried his old persona—what he used to do and who he used to be—I couldn't see all he was becoming. Only after I really forgave him did I notice that my dad had changed. Through forgiveness, I gained new eyes to see. My skewed perception was renewed. I noticed he had changed, as I couldn't realize it before! It was me who was in sin.

He had worked to become more affirming and was excelling in listening, yet I was stuck in the past. Dad had changed, but, before forgiveness, I wouldn't allow him to change in my eyes. I think I lost time in our relationship because of my hard-heartedness and stubbornness. I wish I had forgiven and let go instead of keeping my dad on an old, stinky fishing line.

Now I know. And I will not do that again.

Who are you angry at? Consider forgiving them as Christ has forgiven you. If you can't yet forgive them, ask God to help you. Let the Holy Spirit lead you. Gain understanding from God on the issue. How and why does God call you to forgive? How might you be injuring yourself by not letting the person off the hook?

────── **Prayer** ──────

Father, I am angry, upset, and discouraged. I feel I'm lacking, like others have gotten more, or I just feel angry at people. By Your Spirit, will You come and heal and help me? By Your Spirit, will You set me free? By Your Spirit, will You give me deep and true repentance? I want to meet the equipping power of Your grace in this space. And I thank You that You probably want to heal me even more than I want to be healed. I praise Your name. Worthy are You, King of Kings! Thank You for saving me. Thank You for helping me. I love You! In Jesus's name. Amen.

9

Adopt These Eight Heart Postures

As we have established, hearts think, and hearts—on their own accord—are deceptive. Our hearts dictate our thoughts, our thoughts direct our actions, and our actions determine our lives and whether we follow Jesus or not.

We are spending so much time on our hearts because this is how we welcome in Jesus—and the very mind of Christ (Eph. 3:17). I hope our lives will be ones in which we roll out the red carpet and give Jesus the highest, hugest, and most honorable welcome ever!

Seeking God and seeking a pure heart are part of this process. God tells us, "You will seek me *and find me* when you seek me *with all your heart*" (Jer. 29:13). Deep, hungry, and open hearts welcome Jesus and yield to the mind of Christ.

With this, as we go forward, let's continually evaluate our hearts. And never leave them unattended. The heart requires regular check-ups, just like the physical body. Just as we would never leave our bodies unchecked, clogged, and unhealthy, let's not leave our hearts that way either. There will be no heart attacks on our watch.

Below you will find eight postures of heart designed to help you endure—strong of mind. Each is a declarative statement. The more you say them, the more you'll believe them. This daily habit will help you create new neural pathways in your mind. I have also included a space for journaling at the end of each posture so you can write and reflect.

1. I Trust That God Is Near

It comes down to a matter of trust, doesn't it?

God will save us—or He won't.

God will lead us—or He won't.

God will be with us—or He won't.

Ever noticed? When we think God is not near, we fall into fear. When we think He doesn't care, we start to not care about God. Then we try to achieve perfect results by going at it alone.

"The LORD replied, 'My Presence will go with you, and I will give you rest'" (Exod. 33:14). Rest knows Immanuel, "God with us." Rest gains leniency of heart and room to breathe. Rest is freedom. It knows there is enough grace—outside of legalism, rule-keeping, or self-inflicted demands. Jesus's power really is *truly* perfected through weakness. This is the ultimate form of rest. You can go on a vacation and not be at rest. But when you really trust God and know He has you? That's rest. Rest enters the mental promised lands of God through plains of faith, hope, and love.

My friend, you do not travel alone. There is rest for your soul.

> Have I not commanded you? Be strong and courageous. Do not be afraid; do not be discouraged, for the LORD your God will be with you wherever you go. (Josh. 1:9)

God will help you; He has put His very Spirit inside of you to transform you. If He did it before, as His Word tells us, certainly He can do it again: "The Spirit of the LORD will come powerfully upon you, and you will prophesy with them; and you will be changed into a different person" (1 Sam. 10:6). "Be filled with the [Holy] Spirit and constantly guided by Him" (Eph. 5:18 AMP).

You are never outside of God's guiding Spirit. You are never far from God's helping hand.

God is transforming you into His very image. As you keep your eyes on Him, you will see Him. It pleases God to reveal the Son in you to you (Gal. 1:15–16). "For the creation waits in eager expectation for the children of God to be revealed" (Rom. 8:19).

Say aloud, "I trust God. I trust that God is near."

Journal: God, what does it look like for me to trust You?

---

2. I Don't Need Pity; I Walk in God's Love

There is a story of a woman who was young, smart, and vibrant, but in order to gain a feeling of value, she became an invalid. Maybe she was afraid of getting older. There wasn't much for her to look forward to. Maybe that scared her. Perhaps she considered the years ahead and her impending decline. Or maybe she felt lonely and not worth anything, and she wanted sympathy and empathy from others.

Either way, she decided to just stay in bed. Her old mom came and waited on her hand and foot, carrying food to her room, treating her like a poor old sick person. But one day her mother died. Her time of service was done.

115

The invalid girl struggled at first, lying helpless in her bed. Then she just decided one day to get up, get dressed, and restart her life, right back where she'd ended it.[1] It was as if nothing had happened. She was walking and moving with no issue.

Some of us are invalids because we choose to be. Our insistence that we are stuck and our groanings about being hurt and out of commission keep us stuck. They also bring us sympathy, pity, help, and emotional care from those around us. We become hurt so we can get comfort for our past hurts. So we just stay in bed. We procrastinate. We stay stuck. We don't move. We know human pity but, in this, we do not open ourselves up to receive God's healing love.

Are you groaning? Complaining? Pitying yourself? Crippling yourself? Staying stuck? Waiting things out? Looking for others to sympathize or empathize with your needy heart?

No one ever has gotten better by staying bedridden. No one has experienced light and life by staying under the cover of dark blankets.

People can't give you what only God can. Let the past be the past, and walk into your future, courageously, with God.

Say aloud, "I don't need pity; I walk in God's love."

Journal: Where have I looked to people to give me the pity, comfort, or empathy I should be getting from God? God, how are You trying to reach me with Your love?

3. My Lot in Life Is Beautiful

The devil's demonic plan was to bring himself higher. He said to himself,

> I will ascend to heaven and set my throne above God's
>   stars.
> I will preside on the mountain of the gods
>   far away in the north.
> I will climb to the highest heavens
>   and be like the Most High. (Isa. 14:13–14 NLT)

When I think, *I want what they have. I wish I were that person. I deserve more. I should be more respected. I should be more seen. I wish I were in a better place than where I am today. God should have blessed me. I need to prove myself to get to a higher place,* or when I get critical, slanderous of people, jealous, or envious—I need to check myself before I wreck myself. These thoughts are not of God; many are demonic.

> But if you harbor bitter envy and selfish ambition **in your hearts,** do not boast about it or deny the truth. Such "wisdom" does not come down from heaven but **is earthly, unspiritual, demonic.** For where you have envy and selfish ambition, there you find disorder and every evil practice. (James 3:14–16)

God's Word says,

> In the last days there will be very difficult times. For people will love only themselves and their money. They will be boastful and proud, scoffing at God, disobedient to their parents, and ungrateful. They will consider nothing sacred. They will be unloving and unforgiving; they will slander others and have no self-control. They will be cruel and hate what is good. They will betray their friends, be reckless, be puffed up with pride, and love pleasure rather than God. They

will act religious, but they will reject the power that could make them godly. Stay away from people like that! (2 Tim. 3:1–5 NLT)

The grass is never greener somewhere else. It only looks that way from your lawn. When you hop over your fence and plop yourself smack-dab in the center of someone else's space, you'll see that they have weeds and brown areas too. Many of us look from a distance and think, *They've got it better.* Distance distorts things.

Plus, our grass is the chosen spot for us to meet with God. "The boundary lines have fallen for me in pleasant places; surely I have a delightful inheritance" (Ps. 16:6).

For the longest time, I thought, *I don't want a rented house. I want a house I own.* Then I could decorate. Then I could hang pictures. Then I could plant a garden. But as I sought the Lord, it was like He was saying to me, *Kelly, love your lot.*

So, eventually, I did. I went to the garden center, bought flowers, and planted them all along the front of the house.

There is value in my lot.

It's not that my lot wasn't beautiful; it was just that I kept looking at everyone else's lots on Facebook. Only when I got into seeing the beauty of my own lot did I recognize how blessed I really am. God's presence is right here, where I am. When I look elsewhere, I lose Him. I quickly fall into envy and coveting, which are cardinal sins.

All you ever wanted, and all the goodness God has for you, is right on your own lot.

Say aloud, "My lot in life is beautiful."

Journal: How have I hated my own lot? What goodness might God want me to recognize and give thanks for today?

_____

_____

_____

4. I Have Nothing to Lose by Loving

Yesterday, I saw a woman walking by. When she passed me, she ignored me. *Am I not good enough? What am I, chopped liver?* I thought.

She acted like she didn't know me. This wasn't the first time this had happened.

So I said to her, "Whenever you see me, you don't recognize me." My words had an offended tone in them.

She responded, "Yeah, I can't see very well. I'm getting eye surgery soon."

My wrong assumption drove me to quick accusation. Rather than having a heart to understand her issue, I assumed. And my fleshly instinct was entirely wrong—and judgmental. Even worse, my personal need for acknowledgment—and hatred for rejection—made me into a person I didn't want to be. A person lacking grace.

How are we prone to judge instead of love?

The two don't comingle. Love is patient. Love is kind. Love keeps no record of wrongs. Love covers a multitude of sins. Love listens. Love never fails (1 Cor. 13:4–8).

Judgment points a finger. Finds fault. Proves someone's wrong. Critiques. Hates.

I want to be love, not hate.

If I had known that this friend was getting surgery, I know I would have prayed for her instead of judging her actions. But I didn't know—and that's the point.

We don't always know. In many cases, there is a huge backstory to the quickly formed story we've imagined.

I'm learning it is better to err on the side of compassion. Compassion heals and helps far more than judgment ever will. Is it even possible to give someone too much benefit of the doubt?

We have nothing to lose in love.

Say aloud, "I have nothing to lose by loving."

Journal: How do I resort to judging over loving? How can I respond differently next time?

---

5. God Is Strong in My Weakness

"These people can't skate," I told my brother a couple of months ago, as we glided around the rink. We were having a fun time talking about life, the world, and his job.

I had ice skating down. I'd learned it as a child. My mom got me in lessons early. Even now, visiting a rink I had never been to before in Maryland, and after spending a year off the ice, getting back on was a breeze. In ten minutes, I was flying past people.

But all these other people? What was up with them?

A hockey skater cut me off. An out-of-control ten-year-old lost balance, hung on by one foot, and then flopped in front of me. Another person blocked my exit from the rink because they couldn't stand. *Move out of the way, everyone! I want to fly!*

People were in my way.

Voicing my concerns, I told my brother, "If it weren't *for them,* I'd be all good."

But before I could say anything else, he said, "Kelly, be careful about what you're saying, or soon we'll both fall."

My brother was right: "Pride goes before destruction, a haughty spirit before a fall" (Prov. 16:18). Pride makes people fall.

Yet "the fear of the LORD is the beginning of wisdom" (9:10), and it is wise to "humble yourselves, therefore, under the mighty hand of God so that at the proper time he may exalt you" (1 Pet. 5:6 ESV).

Pride relies just as much on its own strength as it fears its own weakness. With pride, there are two sides to the coin. It's easy to feel arrogant when doing well and stupid when struggling.

For instance, I thought I had to be a super strong writer when writing this book. I knew I wasn't really doing that great. I felt frustrated by my lack at times. I wanted my words and sentences to be perfect. The Lord had to stop me in my tracks with a heart nudge. *Kelly, don't use this book to validate or esteem yourself. That's not what I have for you.*

His prompt was right. My job isn't to please you (although I have been praying this book sets you free). My job is to please Him. In this, I am not bound by anyone's like or dislike; I am tied to Jesus. His yoke is easy and His burden is light (Matt. 11:30). His opinion is the one that matters.

So, I said, "God, even my worst words with Your Word are the best words! *You* will powerfully change people's worlds through Your Word."

And I released both my pride and my weakness to Him. With none of me and all of Him, God can, and still will, do everything. I trust Him apart from me. His power is not perfected through my words or wisdom, through my best moves or my worst. No, His power is sent out through my willing weakness, ever submitted to His power. It is all of God and none of me.

What about you? Are you relying on your strength or His? Are you trying to prop up your ego or pursuing His name?

God needs none of you for all of Him to work on your behalf. That's grace. As you move out of His way, He moves. God has this! He has you!

Say aloud, "God is strong in my weakness."

Journal: What am I relying on to give me security or significance apart from God? How does my weakness make me feel insecure? How can I shift from trusting me to trusting God?

6. Right Now, I Put All My Trust in God

Jeremiah 17:6 says those who put their trust in other people "will live in the barren wilderness" (NLT). I remember a time where I thought I'd made a new best friend. I had just gotten to know the woman. She was sure to be an amazing friend. We were off to a fast friendship. I loved hearing what she had to say, and I sure hoped I was blessing her too. Excited about all our conversations and what God was doing, I dreamed of doing ministry together. It seemed God was using her in a big way—why not me and her? So, to put it lightly, I prayed heavily that we would do ministry together. I walked the hallways and called out to God. I expressed to her my *big* vision and encouraged her to move on it. And then the carpet got pulled out from under me. She disappeared on me.

Was I not good enough? Did I say something wrong? What happened to my dream? Later, I had to face the fact that I was barren because I'd put my trust in the wrong thing. I was looking for her to do what only God is meant to do. "This is what the LORD says: 'Cursed are those *who put their trust in mere humans*'" (v. 5 NLT).

My heart got so caught up in the ministry idea that I never leaned on the mind of Christ to make sure He was 100 percent in it. If I had sought to ask Him, I may have discovered His real heart. Maybe He was for the ministry idea, but not with this woman. Maybe He had a friendship for me with this woman, but no ministry. Maybe I'd have a friendship with this woman, and I'd bring up the ministry to her ten years later. But because I was so set on my plan, and because I put my trust in her to accomplish it, I think God allowed this friend to be removed from my life. That hurt.

But I learned.

> Cursed [with great evil] is the strong man who trusts in and relies on frail man, making weak [human] flesh his arm, and whose **mind and heart** turn aside from the Lord.
>
> For he shall be like a shrub or a person naked and destitute in the desert; and **he shall not see any good come**, but shall dwell in the parched places in the wilderness, in an uninhabited salt land. (vv. 5–6 AMPC)

I was left barren because I trusted the wrong maker. To believe another person can be our maker is the making of ruin. We have only one Maker: God our Father. If we put our trust in God, His Word says we will not "be put to shame" (Ps. 25:3).

Where are you looking to others to give you what only God can? Where are you demanding that people do better or be better for you? How are you expecting things to get better only if someone else does?

Skip the path I took. There is only One worthy of all our hearts' trust, reliance, belief, hope, and confidence. And, best of all, rather than barrenness, He has blessing for you as you trust Him:

> [Most] blessed is the man who believes in, trusts in, and relies on the Lord, and whose hope and confidence the Lord is.
> For he shall be like a tree planted by the waters that spreads out its roots by the river; and it shall not see and fear when heat comes; but its leaf shall be green. It shall not be anxious and full of care in the year of drought, nor shall it cease yielding fruit. (Jer. 17:7–8 AMPC)

What do you want, fruit or loneliness? Vitality or barrenness? Deep roots or shallow striving?

In prior years, when I have been attacked, I have made what I call Jewelry Cards of Truth. I write verses on note cards to combat what I am dealing with most. Then I store them in my jewelry box. These truths are treasure. When I feel attacked, I grab them and speak them over my life. If you are struggling with putting others before your Maker, perhaps you can search out your own jewelry card verses. Here are a few to get you going:

> Don't put your trust in mere humans.
> They are as frail as breath.
> What good are they? (Isa. 2:22 NLT)

No one can serve two masters. Either you will hate the one and love the other, or you will be devoted to the one and despise the other. You cannot serve both God and money. (Matt. 6:24)

> Some trust in chariots and some in horses,
> but we trust in the name of the LORD our God. (Ps. 20:7)

Say aloud, "Right now, I put all my trust in God."

Journal: How have you trusted in other people more than your Maker? What would it look like for you to trust God first and foremost?

7. I Forgive Me!

Last night, I was dumbstruck by my own thoughts. Out of nowhere, I told myself, *Kelly, you're bad.* In that moment, I wanted to hit myself. For a girl who decades ago struggled with an eating disorder (and was freed from it!), this moment was scary—terrifying, even. *What's going on with me?*

I made a mistake, yes. But what was I going to do, hate myself forever for it?

I knew I needed to forgive myself, but I hated myself so much for what I'd done that I couldn't. The sin wouldn't stop convicting and condemning me no matter how much I repented. I got a headache. I became short-tempered. I needed to get away from everyone, but I couldn't.

Unforgiveness toward self is how bad cycles plague families. For instance, by continuing to feel and respond in shame, it is super easy to shame one's kids. Then the kids feel bad and retaliate back with shame. When they feel shame, they shame the parent, and then the parent feels bad and does the same. It is an endless gerbil wheel.

Only when we forgive ourselves do we stop the cycle. To do this we must remember that we are *worthy*. We must go back to the truth: we *are* completely unworthy, but *Jesus*.

Even if we can't receive our own worthiness—either way, it doesn't matter—we don't earn forgiveness by proving to be the most worthy person in the nation. Likewise, we don't lose it by being the least worthy person. Christ is our worth, and we are now His possession. We are redeemed and forgiven, completely independent of our bad actions.

God is that good. He forgives in a split second, entirely forgetting our wrongs.

Do you feel it is hard to forgive yourself? What if you were to rely on the price Jesus paid for you on the cross?

In my situation, I closed my eyes. I remembered Jesus getting beaten on the cross. Whip after whip. Insult after insult. He took it all—for me. He took the beating to release me from beating myself up. He defeated sin's power entirely on the cross. He fully defeated shame.

This is love. Every hit He took absorbed all my sin, wrongs, mistakes—all my shame. His sacrifice is more than enough to release me from what I can't release myself from.

I opened my heart to receive and hear the mind of Christ, and I felt He wanted me to understand, *Kelly, I did this for you—for this moment you are experiencing right here, right now. . . . But, Kelly, do you believe the cross is enough? Can you receive what I've done, for you, in this moment, right now?*

Do you believe the cross is enough? By His wounds we are healed, helped, and delivered from bad cycles.

> But he was pierced for our transgressions,
>   he was crushed for our iniquities;
>   the punishment **that brought us peace** was on him,
>   and by his wounds we are healed. (Isa. 53:5)

Say aloud, "I forgive me!"

Journal: What sin, condemnation, or accusation keeps pestering you? Have you repented of it? What does it look like for you to receive God's forgiveness?

8. My Problem Is Not Too Big for God

Remember our car ride in North Carolina where we nearly drove off the mountain—but God? Well, finally—thanks to God—we made it to our destination and pulled into the parking lot to prepare for our long mountain hike. We sprayed ourselves with tick repellent and bundled up to prepare for the high ascent on this cool winter day. The sun was bright as we started to climb, but the rocks were wet and slippery. I tried to walk daintily up the mountain, but I like looking at things. Sometimes when we walk, I lag behind, then realize it and have to run to catch up. Along this particular journey, we crawled over big boulders. I was sure I was going to fall, but I kept my eyes peeled ahead and, after an hour, with various pit stops for water, we made it to the top.

The view was astounding! We could see for miles and miles, over the tops of mountains that looked like hills, and trees that looked like toothpicks. We breathed in the light air. We celebrated our win, and the view was our reward.

While we were standing on the tallest mountain in the area, one that made me feel on top of the world, my daughter spoke up. "From up here, all the other mountains we see in the distance are small."

Her words struck me, reminding me of this verse: "Truly I tell you, if you have faith as small as a mustard seed, you can say to this mountain, 'Move from here to there,' and it will move. Nothing will be impossible for you" (Matt. 17:20).

From God's view, as He sees from His high mountain, all mountains are small. Very small. They aren't hard to move but easy.

The problem for us humans is that when we look at our problems, we see them from a lateral view instead of a high view. Yet if we are able to see our problems from a high view—to exchange our view for God's view—we see from a place of greater faith. We see the escape routes. We understand the lay of the land. We can see what else is coming over the horizon.

How can you move your heart and emotions above your problem? How can you exalt God your Father and Christ your Savior over your problem? How can you be expectant for what He will do as you let go of fear and worry?

Mountains become small in light of God's equipping and enabling power.

Say aloud, "My problem is not too big for God."

Journal: What mountain is in front of you? What looks too hard to conquer? How might taking a higher view help you see more?

PART 3

Start Now: Take Every Thought Captive

10

The Stop/Start Process

Sow a thought, reap an action; sow an action, reap a habit; sow a habit, reap a character; sow a character, reap a destiny.

Stephen Covey, *The 7 Habits of Highly Effective People*

We reap what we sow. If we sow good thoughts, we will reap a good life. To sow good thoughts, we guard them. We take captive thoughts so we can be captivated by the King and His beauty. To take every thought captive, we must stop having hindering thoughts and start to agree with God. Said another way, we:

1. *Stop* thinking according to our conformed minds.
2. *Start* thinking according to our renewed minds.

A conformed mind is led by old ways and by the enemy's lies. It places pleasing people above pleasing God. It goes after comfort before connection with God. It falls back into old patterns instead of receiving strength to endure and persevere in forming new ones.

Ungodliness cannot produce godliness. This is why we must *stop* the old to *start* something new.

No one ever says, "I am going to set out today to get myself stuck in a horrible pit that I can't climb out of!" It is insidious thoughts that lead them into pits. More than likely they didn't intend to cheat on their spouse, become a drug addict, or wreck their family and drown their sorrows in vodka.

These things do not happen overnight—they happen thought-by-thought, step-by-step. The first thought may be, *I can't handle life.* The second may be, *I have to handle this feeling.* The third becomes, *I don't know how.* Over the course of a year, or two, or four, the thought once drowned out by a glass of bourbon now requires a whole bottle. Thoughts keep going—and actions progress—until and unless they are stopped.

Which is why the Stop/Start Process we are about to go into is mission critical. We *stop* ungodly thought patterns to *start* aligning to the mind of Christ.

This simple two-part process is easy to apply to any thought that is plaguing you, tormenting you, beating you down, castrating your purpose, confusing your mind, destroying your confidence, disturbing your peace, or whatever else.

You can return to this chapter until you get the whole process down. You can use this methodology on any thought you come in contact with. As you'll see in coming chapters, I will tease out the process. I do this so you can learn how to apply it to any thought you may be facing. You will learn how to do it through example.

Foundational Elements

Before you get into the application of the Stop/Start Process, it is important to know it is founded on three things:

1. The Holy Spirit
2. The Word of God (truth)
3. Discerning prayer

Without these, the effectiveness of this process wanes. With them, you will not want for the mind of Christ; it will own your mind.

1. The Holy Spirit

The Holy Spirit reveals and walks us into all truth (John 16:13), shows Christ in us and to us (vv. 14–15), leads us (Matt. 4:1; Rom. 8:14), empowers us (Luke 4:14; 24:49), fills us (Acts 2:4; Eph. 5:18), affirms we're God's children (Rom. 8:16), yields fruit in us (Gal. 5:22), renews us (Titus 3:5), searches all things to reveal the deep things of God to us (1 Cor. 2:10), speaks to us and through us and through others (Matt. 10:20; John 1:33; 14:26; 1 Cor. 12:3; Heb. 3:7), convicts us of sin (John 16:7–8), enlightens our eyes (Eph. 1:17), and so much more.

What I try to do regularly when approaching my thoughts is to invite the Holy Spirit into the process. I ask God, "Father, by Your Holy Spirit, will You reveal and heal? Will You illuminate and speak to me? Will You bring clarity in what to stop and what to start by Your power? Will You give me eyes to see and ears to hear what You, the Holy Spirit, are saying?"

Then I listen to what the Spirit is saying.

Paul, in the Bible, did this too. Paul said, "For it *seemed good* to the Holy Spirit and to us to lay no greater burden on you than these few requirements" (Acts 15:28 NLT).

Paul was able to identify what seemed good to the Holy Spirit through discerning. He also said, "And *now I know* that none of you to whom I have preached the Kingdom will ever see me again" (20:25 NLT).

How did Paul know this? By the Holy Spirit, by the very mind of Christ, he had a "knowing."

We can know by the Spirit, too, just like Paul, by God's doing. This is why the Holy Spirit is so imperative to taking our every thought captive. We want His mind, not our own. We want to be such a pure vessel that we are sensitive to the Holy Spirit and not quenching Him.

All this makes me think about one girl I counseled. She had horrific problems with her family. At times, I had no words to speak. I didn't know what to say or how to lead her. All I knew to do was to pray. I prayed, "Come, Holy Spirit, and help!" And after that, a wellspring of wisdom and insight surfaced that I could share with her. She got answers and breakthrough. She began to see that through her own breaking, God wasn't ruining her but making her into His image.

This wisdom was not from me; it was all the Holy Spirit.

Always welcome the Holy Spirit, before you even begin the Stop/Start Process.

Pray, "Father, thank You for the Holy Spirit. I ask the Holy Spirit to come, to fill me with a spirit of wisdom and revelation, counsel, might, knowledge, and fear of the Lord. May there be a great revealing as I go through this process, by Your Spirit. May I yield and submit to the mind of Christ. In Jesus's name. Amen."

2. The Word of God

This Word is not a light fluff-piece. It is a glory force with a proven track record of awe-inspiring testimonies, faith-filled conquests, and triumphs.

When using the Word, we don't just read it and think passing thoughts about it but wield it until it becomes so much a part of us we become it. We wage war with it until demonic and fleshly things vanish before us. We let it operate on us to the point that our hearts are restructured and renewed. We cut down strongholds with it, giving free passage to Christ's heart.

"In the beginning was the Word, and the Word was with God, and the Word was God" (John 1:1). The Word is not only words on paper; the Word is Jesus, Himself.

The Word is His Word to us. Just as we would give someone our word, this is God's Word. And when His Word becomes our word, we cannot go wrong.

For the Word that God speaks is alive and full of power [making it active, operative, energizing, and effective]; it is sharper than any two-edged sword, penetrating to the dividing line of the breath of life (soul) and [the immortal] spirit, and of joints and marrow [of the deepest parts of our nature], exposing and sifting and analyzing and judging the very thoughts and purposes of the heart. (Heb. 4:12 AMPC)

The Word of God, like a hammer or a sword, cuts Christ into us and our flesh out of us. The Word of God is energizing, empowering, equipping, and engaging. The Word of God is operative. It does surgery to remove what will kill us. It then reorients and rehabs us. Our priorities are reset and recalibrated. And this is where we are activated in mind, word, and deed.

The Word has the power to not only change what is within us but everything around us. It breathes life just as God breathed life into the world, by His Spirit. As we overflow with the Living Word, the Word makes life live in our world.

"'Is not my word like fire,' declares the LORD, 'and like a hammer that breaks a rock in pieces?'" (Jer. 23:29).

Friend, do you have a mental barrier before you that cannot be broken? Who cares what you see?

I encourage you right now to not be taken aback by that thing. Faith is the substance of things hoped for. Know that the Word of God, the sword of the Spirit, is powerful enough. With an earthly sword one can surely kill unruly flesh or wound an opposing warrior. With the Word of God? What can't you do? Hit that thing with the sword of the Spirit and shatter it. Do you have strongholds? Break them down. Do you have snakes in your mind you can't smoke out? God's Word will be the fire.

I pray you gain understanding of the power you hold in God's Word. Everything moves in response to it. Nothing can stop a son or daughter living by His Word instead of their own mind. One hundred percent—you will win battles with the sword of the Spirit, the Word of God, as your weapon.

The Word is power. We are well armed, always, when we hold God's Word near and dear!

Wimps don't carry swords; warriors do. Get up and go to war. Be strong in the power of His might as you prepare to go through this two-part process. Write down verses included in this book. You are equipped. You have all you need, mighty warrior.

Set your will on His will.

Set your truth on His truth.

Set your eyes on His eyes.

Set your heart on His heart.

Do these things so much that His Word is your Word in spirit, mind, and truth. And His Son becomes alive and working in and through you.

3. Discerning Prayer

"Don't act thoughtlessly, but understand what the Lord wants you to do" (Eph. 5:17 NLT). Praying is seeking understanding. When we pray, we are not to doubt but receive (Mark 11:24; James 1:6–8). Receiving is the posture of discerning what God would have us to do. It is understanding what the Spirit is saying. Is He calling us to wait on Him, or is He leading us to get going? Is He encouraging us to pray more or to take a risky step of love?

Love doesn't operate by its own mind but by the mind of Christ.

Through the Stop/Start Process, wise people pray continuously. They discern what God would have them do and understand what the Spirit is saying.

Don't just talk at God; pray and receive from Him. Jesus said, "He who has ears [to hear], let him be listening and let him consider and perceive and comprehend by hearing" (Matt. 13:9 AMPC).

Through listening, considering, perceiving, and continual seeking, we uncover what God is saying and revealing. It is both attentiveness and intentionality that move us beyond the natural and into the spiritual. There is a shift here. We go somewhere new. Then prayer removes hindrances, diversions, and distractions so we can see clearly. Not all can see.

Jesus also said, "Therefore I speak to them in parables; because while seeing they do not see, and while hearing they do not hear, nor do they understand" (v. 13 NASB). Many could not understand Jesus's stories because they lacked eyes to see. Likewise, many could not see Jesus because they expected Him to come another way. I don't know about you, but I don't want to have my mind blocked and miss love made manifest, Jesus, when He is right before me.

We either see problems or we see Jesus. It is hard to focus on both at the same time. When we see Jesus, who is love, we love those around us.

His mind becomes our mind in large part through prayer, submitting to His will. Then, through understanding and clarity, His course becomes ours. As we come to the Way, He makes a way. He leads; we follow. Remember, we are Christ followers. Our procession is not just in word but through action. The mind of Christ leads in this.

The Nitty Gritty: Applying the Stop/Start Process

Let's dig in. In the chapters to come, we will apply the Stop/Start Process to five common thoughts that bug children of God. What you need to know is these five thoughts are just examples, which you personally may or may not struggle with. That doesn't so much matter. What does matter is that you learn the process so you can apply it to any thought, at any time, with great success. Working through these examples will help you be able to do that.

As I mentioned earlier, I encourage you to pray first and welcome the Holy Spirit. Then get some paper or a journal and go through the process. Writing helps with remembering. If you go through the process one day and find yourself in the same pit another day, you can return to your notes. It's amazing how much we can forget in a day.

I also recommend starting a specific "take thoughts captive" journal (or download the free "Two-Step Stop/Start Worksheet" at www.itakethoughtscaptive.com to assist you). Either way, keep returning to what you are learning. Learning solidifies truth. So does repetitively declaring God's Word; it rewires our minds.

Let's begin with part 1 of the process.

Part 1: STOP

To stop means we STOP. In this step, the goal is to *think about what we're thinking about*. It is to notice what our minds are saying. Here, if a thought is not of God's heart, if it is full of pride or if it is blatant sin—we can apprehend it like an intruder. In this process we are the enforcement agents; our thoughts are the captives who must obey Christ.

Our job is to only let in "whatever is true, whatever is noble, whatever is right, whatever is pure, whatever is lovely, whatever is admirable—if anything is excellent or praiseworthy—think about such things" (Phil. 4:8). If our thought is a violator, or seemingly good but still an intruder (pride, fear, worry, self-protective, or self-defeating), we also take it down. We bring it to the ground and make it obedient to Christ.

The goal is to STOP intruding thoughts. No longer will they violate and desecrate our minds.

1. Capture the Thought

If there is an intruder at your house, you have to capture them before you can boot them out. This step is all about apprehending the intruding thought.

138

Here, we may feel a feeling. Sometimes we don't even begin with the conscious thought but with a feeling. Why? Because feelings often produce thoughts. This is why it is important to note what we feel first. Feelings are predictors of thoughts to come. They are indicators of internal struggles.

For example, if we feel anxious or overwhelmed, we have to work backward to identify what subconscious thought is behind our feeling.

The goal is to get down to the exact thought that is pestering you. Perhaps, in identifying the thought, you will get to, "I am under so much pressure to get my work done by 5:00 today."

Then ask yourself, *What belief is under this thought and feeling?* Discern what the Holy Spirit may be saying. "For God does speak—now one way, now another—though no one perceives it" (Job 33:14).

It is important to perceive the belief underlying the feeling and thought. Why? Because belief is the foundation of thought.

For instance, if I believe I am secure in driving over a bridge because it is sturdy and strong, I will not be afraid of doing so. But if I believe it is shaky or about to crumble, I will drive over it with fear and timidity. Beliefs dictate our thoughts and our approach.

Beliefs tell a mind how to go. They dictate actions. They drive a person to peace or to pull out their hair. And so not only our thoughts but also our wrong beliefs must be brought into submission to Christ.

In this step, write down any feelings, thoughts, or beliefs that need to be captured and note what the Holy Spirit reveals to you as you pray.

Then prepare to identify who is speaking to you.

2. Determine Who Is Speaking

In the second STOP step, we figure out who is speaking this thought over us.

Is it God whispering in a still, small voice? God comes with faith, hope, and love. His kingdom is founded on righteousness, peace, and joy. When God speaks, these attributes are often present. When following the mind of Christ, followers find peace. Why? Because Jesus is the Prince of Peace. To follow Him is to go to destination peace.

Is it the enemy, the accuser of your soul, speaking? The devil speaks no truth. He is the coordinator and orchestrator of all lies; he is the father of lies (John 8:44). He is a murderer. When the enemy talks in your mind, you will hear lies about yourself, lies about others—assumptions, presumptions, arguments, judgments, nonsense, rebuttals, condemnation, and conspiracies about things and people—and lies about your future.

If a thought in your head assassinates someone's character, that's a red flag. If it questions if God really has good things for you, sound an alarm. If a thought convinces you that you're out of God's love, let a siren sound. If a thought comes to say, *There's no hope*, that is a huge indicator the enemy is on the loose. And if a thought causes you to sin, that is a big "Whoa!" moment. "The wages of sin is death" (Rom. 6:23). Where the devil comes to kill, Jesus is life. After recognizing God is not speaking, we always have the ability to shift back to God's Word, truth, and life.

Is it the flesh speaking in your mind? The flesh is full of lusts, appetites, and desires. It sounds like, *I should have . . . I need to . . . People should . . . I really deserve . . .*

Flesh thinks about me, myself, and I—as *numero uno* of importance. It also perpetuates sin and pride. It thinks its way is the best, and it operates in self-reliance and self-dependence instead of God-dependence. It exalts its own way above love. It seeks its own promotion and is driven by selfish ambition. Jealousy, coveting, or self-centeredness pop up when the flesh exerts itself.

People who operate from thoughts of the flesh tend to find themselves confused, disoriented, demotivated, angry, bitter, discouraged, down, and in a bubble of their own self-consumption.

They pursue entertainment and comfort more than being dead to themselves and alive to Christ.

Who is speaking? Which of these three voices is talking in your mind? If you follow the destroyer, your life will be destroyed. If you follow your flesh, your life will be self-centered and nothing more. If you follow Jesus, you will find the way, the truth, and the life and have life in abundance.

Which will you choose?

3. Understand Intent

When a captor is apprehended and brought in, the law enforcement team seeks to understand intent and the implications of that intent. Here, we want to do similarly.

For instance, if you were able to realize that the thought was from the devil, you may ask yourself, *What did the devil want to steal, kill, or destroy through this thought?*

I have noticed that the devil often tries to stop something God has for me to do. The devil is famous in my life for coming with distractions so I don't follow the mind of Christ's intent to love through me. If I get pulled off track with duties or obligations, I quickly forget my good intentions. The devil quickly destroys God-prompted action through my inaction.

The second question in this part is to ask, *If this thought (distraction, in my case) is left unchecked, in five, ten, or thirty years, where will it lead me?*

Distraction leads us to a displeasing life. If I am distracted, I'll be pulled every direction. I'll be double-minded. I'll be left discouraged without an aim in life.

To know who is speaking and what they're saying is to see where that voice wants to take us. Seeing where we are going is a great help, because we can decide if we really want to go there. If that destination is not Christ-centric, we have all power, through Christ, to adjust course and to start listening to the right voice: the mind of Christ.

The mind of Christ, His Word, and His Holy Spirit will not lead us wrong, even if it appears all wrong to our natural minds.

This is the STOP process. Like a law enforcement agent, you first capture the thought, then you determine who is responsible for it, and finally you discover its intent and the implications if it is left unchecked.

To know your enemy and to capture him is half the battle when taking your thoughts captive.

The other half is starting. It's like rehabilitation for a mind.

Part 2: START

Now that we know what we must stop doing, we must start doing something new.

So, how does START break down practically?

1. Submit to the Mind of Christ

We must rehabilitate our thoughts. In rehabilitation, people relearn who they are. *We are sons and daughters of God.* They also need to know they're safe. "The name of the LORD is a strong tower" (Prov. 18:10 ESV). *We are going to be okay.*

How do we move who we are, and how are we protected as we move from a mind concept to heart ownership? We do this by *adoring the King!* We acknowledge, declare, and praise who God is. We say things like, "Jesus, You are King. You are the head of Your body. You are our ruler. You are our just judge. You are Lord of my life; I surrender to You again." We agree with His verdicts. We submit to His lordship. We tell our minds what to believe until the new truth is rooted deeply.

We also *renew our minds in the Word of God.* We read the Bible to find out what God says about our thought. We read stories of people who may have had the same struggle. We prime the pump with God's oil and write down His truth. We also seek, through prayer, God's wisdom about the thought; we discern what the mind of Christ is revealing and saying. We let His truth speak louder than our lie.

What does this look like? After adoring the King, seek the Word and write down the truths that speak louder than your lie. Pray and ask God to help you receive His truth. Listen to His heart. Journal with God. Turn that truth list into declarative statements. Begin, daily, to declare them over yourself. For example, "[I am part of] a chosen people, a royal priesthood" (1 Pet. 2:9).

2. Discover Any Unlocked Doors

The second START step helps you to identify what unlocked and opened this thought in your mind.

Ask yourself the following questions:

- *What may have opened me up to feel this way?* A show? A friend? A situation? A boundary I let down? A book?
- *What is under my thought?* Fear? Rejection? Anger? Bitterness?
- *Is there something in my history I need to repent of?* Something that keeps coming to mind?

Without handling the root, you'll continually experience the fruit. But if you know the root, you can remove it. For instance, if a show left you restless and afraid, don't watch it again. That's uprooting it.

3. Repent, Renounce, and Pray

To relock those doors, we first need to repent of sin. Sin is not a light and fluffy pet we keep with us. It is a violating issue to the temple of God that needs to be booted out. After doing this, we must break agreements with anything that is not truth. Say, "I do agree that I ____. I break agreement with the lie that ____. I renounce (pride, arrogance, doubt, fear, etc.)." At this point you may also say, "I recommit my eyes, my heart, my hands, and my thinking—the whole of me—to You, God. I want all of me to be in line with Your Word and Your mind. This day, I let go of my ways for Yours. I give You my eye-gate, ear-gate, and mouth-gate. I am Your temple. I am holy in Your sight. I pray all I am will bring You glory and honor. I surrender afresh. I trust You, God. In Jesus's name. Amen."

4. Go a New Way

Rehabilitation restores our brokenness to newness of life. We walk in new life-giving habits that replace old bad habits. We stop doing what we used to do, lest it lure our minds again. A curious dog returns to smell its own poo. *Yuck.* Let's not be that dog.

So often in Scripture, it is written that Jesus gives us one thing for another. Take a look:

> The Spirit of the Sovereign LORD is on me,
>   because the LORD has anointed me
>   to proclaim good news to the poor.
> He has sent me to bind up the brokenhearted,
>   to proclaim freedom for the captives
>   and release from darkness for the prisoners,
> to proclaim the year of the LORD's favor
>   and the day of vengeance of our God,
> to comfort all who mourn,
>   and provide for those who grieve in Zion—
> to bestow on them a crown of beauty
>   instead of ashes,
> the oil of joy
>   instead of mourning,
> and a garment of praise
>   instead of a spirit of despair. (Isa. 61:1–3)

This may sound odd. Forceful, even—to presume a different feeling—but I have noticed that when I do the opposite of what my thought was trying to get me to do (especially a demonically sourced thought), I can experience radical breakthrough and *stop* that neural track from cutting a deeper rut.

For instance, if I find myself judging my husband, instead I can heed Scripture and start blessing him in my mind. I don't have to submit to a critical spirit or justify why I am doing it. I can bless my own house instead of tearing it down.

> Never return evil for evil or insult for insult (scolding, tongue-lashing, berating), but on the contrary blessing [praying for their welfare, happiness, and protection, and truly pitying and loving them]. For know that to this you have been called, that you may yourselves inherit a blessing [from God—that you may obtain a blessing as heirs, bringing welfare and happiness and protection]. (1 Pet. 3:9 AMPC)

If I am feeling lonely or sad, I can thank Jesus for all He has done for me. Then, practically, I can smile and feel it real deep in my soul. Something shifts.

We can choose, in many ways, how to act. Life is less about what happens to us and more about how we respond to it. In this, I think it is very possible to move into joy instead of mourning, praise instead of despair, and beauty instead of ashes.

It's not always as hard as we make it seem or as hard as the enemy tells us it is. Jesus has afforded us a lot; the enemy wants us to forget that.

God honors faith-filled actions. Think: sometimes the hardest part about getting going is just getting the bike moving. Once it starts, it keeps rolling along.

The key is to ask God, "What does my new way look like for me?" Be open to the Comforter, the Holy Spirit, in the process. Don't just stop the thought; do a new thing. By the mind of Christ, replace the old thought. Consider how Jesus would set forth in faith, hope, and love. Move accordingly.

5. Keep the Temple Shining

Above all else—guard that heart! Mind your mind. How do you do this?

- *Pray* for protection. Pray that God would keep you from evil and that you could stay on guard. Then use discernment going forward.
- *Think* on what is good. Think about what you are thinking about. Think about what you are thinking about others. Think about what the mind of Christ is leading you to think about.
- *Keep using* the sword of the Spirit and lift up the shield of faith.

Swords are used for advancement. Shields are used for protection. Use the sword of the Spirit to advance. Use the shield of God's promises to protect your heart. God is always true to His Word. And He is faithful to His Word to perform it.

> So is my word that goes out from my mouth:
>   It will not return to me empty,
> but will accomplish what I desire
>   and achieve the purpose for which I sent it. (Isa. 55:11)

A Note about the Two-Part Stop/Start Process

This process may seem like a lot. But it shouldn't feel so intricate after you practice using it a couple of times. After you use it on a few thoughts, your mind will get the process down. Like automatic moving gears, you'll advance through each step with ease. Remember, you can easily return to this chapter for review. A smart thing to do is to place a note card, perhaps on your computer or bathroom mirror, that will help you remember each step of the process.

STOP
1. Capture the Thought
2. Determine Who Is Speaking
3. Understand Intent

START
1. Submit to the Mind of Christ
2. Discover Any Unlocked Doors
3. Repent, Renounce, and Pray
4. Go a New Way
5. Keep the Temple Shining

In the coming chapters, you will see how to use this method to address any thought. Your life is about to powerfully change—for the better. To mind your mind is to walk with the mind of Christ!

——— **Free Download** ———

Find the "Take Every Thought Captive Worksheet" at www.itakethoughtscaptive.com. This worksheet will help you journal through the two-part Stop/Start Process of taking every thought captive.

11

Break Down the Lie of "I Am Not Enough or Don't Have Enough"

The grace of God means something like: "Here is your life. You might never have been, but you *are*, because the party wouldn't have been complete without you."

Frederick Buechner, *Wishful Thinking*

I just learned that a 1900s Ball Mason jar with the brand name inscribed upside down could get someone $1,000. And apparently a Superman lunch box could get you $16,000. Old postcards? $50,000.[1] Who would have thought? Yet, the funny part is, some people seeing one of those old things on a counter would call it trash! I know I would probably just toss those things out if I came across them in an attic. What we don't realize has value, we trash.

Many people own things of incredible value yet throw them out because they don't know their worth.

You are incredibly valuable, but do you trash yourself? You are incredibly worthy in God's eyes, but are you hard on you? You are a treasure of great measure, but do you negate how God has made you? You are a temple of the Lord, but do you hate your body? Maybe you feel like you're not enough.

Today, I hopped in my white SUV and headed out to the grocery store, just going through my day. I pulled up to a stop sign, singing to music as I drove. I felt happy. But at the stop sign, a man in the car next to me gave me a dirty look. I felt bad. Why was he upset? I didn't do anything wrong, did I? I wondered, *Did I not come to a complete stop? Did I mess up? Is there something wrong with me?*

Some of us feel God looks at us with a glaring face too. As if He is searching for what is wrong with us instead of what is right. Maybe He is upset because we're always late, not godly enough, not smart enough, not good enough, not pretty enough, not doing enough, or not biblical enough?

Some of us feel that the world looks at us like this too. Do others think our butts are too big, the way we talk is too loud, the amount of time we need by ourselves is just odd, or the way we go about things is not right? Their sideways glances can send us subliminal messages: *You are not enough. What is wrong with you?*

How do you feel judged? How do you have to uphold a standard to feel okay about yourself? There are many thoughts that can make us feel not enough, like we are lacking in a particular department. Some prevalent ones are:

I'm too late.

I'm not smart enough.

I'm behind others.

I'm fatally flawed.

I'm held back.

I'm not equipped.

I have to prove myself to others.

I must perform to feel good.

I'm not where I should be.

I don't have enough material items, power, or status.

Applying the Stop/Start Process

The lie we are going to address is: *I am not enough, so I must prove myself to others.*

One day, I invited a beautiful group of friends over for the morning. Everything had to be flawless. I arranged the display of colorful salads and tea cookies to look just right in my porcelain bowls. The water, in a big jug, had sliced cucumbers and lime in it. I double-inspected the house for any dirt or dust. Everything was planned down to the minute in my head. We would sit down at 9:10, after people caught up for ten minutes. We would eat for forty minutes. I would do an introductory welcome for five minutes. My heart raced with all the planning and envisioning of how things would turn out (aka worrying). Every place setting had a pretty napkin. Everything smelled beautiful. Flowers and blankets were set nearby for each person. I wanted immense beauty. Every minute was planned in terms of what I would say. Every song was set, ready to go on a playlist.

I hoped all this would be enough. Would my guests want to come back again? Would they want me? Would what I did be enough? Would I be enough? Wise enough? Good enough?

Nervousness gripped my insides. My heart felt a little twisted, and my heartbeat was faster than it should be. All during the event I was wondering, *How am I doing? Do they like it? Will they want me after this?*

After it ended, I criticized everything I did. *It didn't go well enough. I should have done things differently. I didn't do a good enough job.*

151

Let's begin to work through this scenario with our two-part process as it pertains to this situation and my thought.

STOP

1. Capture the Thought

In this case, feelings of pressure were intruding on my peace. Pressure and worry were making me focus more on aesthetics than on God and His purpose for the morning.

I experienced strong feelings of panic and stress. What were my thoughts? My thoughts were: *I have to be good. I may not be wanted based on how I performed. I didn't do a good enough job.*

I had underlying beliefs, a level below these invasive thoughts, that included: *I have to perform perfectly to be loved. My worth is dependent on what I do and how I look. I have to be more or project more than simply how God made me.*

2. Determine Who Is Speaking

Would God tell me that I am not enough? No. He says I am His workmanship (Eph. 2:10 ESV). That means I already am beautiful and enough, just as I am. This thought was not the voice of God.

Was it the devil speaking, getting under my skin? Hmm. Maybe. The devil is known for getting people to try to prove themselves. Remember when he tried to get Jesus to prove Himself in the wilderness various times? Jesus didn't have to prove anything; He was *already* the Son of God. He didn't need to turn a rock into bread or to throw Himself down to see if an angel would lift Him up. Jesus was loved, wanted, chosen—and He knew it, because the Father had just spoken His identity over Him before He went into the wilderness. When the devil tried to get Him to prove, show off, or make a big scene (Luke 4:1–13), Jesus didn't fall for it.

I didn't have to either. This biblical story sounds like my own in many ways: I am already loved. I am already wanted. The devil may poke with a pitchfork, but I don't have to move. Just because the devil tries to compete with God doesn't mean I have to join his party. I'm already enough. I don't work for God's approval; I have rest when I live from it.

Now, what about my flesh? Was this thought Mrs. Kelly Balarie speaking? Oh yes. There is much to do with my flesh here. When we worry about looking good or appearing just right, flesh is talking. When appearances are front and center, flesh is exerting its muscle.

Flesh tries to drive us from *our wants*; the Holy Spirit moves us according to what *God wants*. The two are galaxies apart. How can I love God with all my heart, all my soul, all my strength, and all my mind when my flesh demands to be loved and serviced?

3. Understand Intent

What was the intent? I can see now that the enemy's intent in this situation was to steal joy. He probably wanted my mind so focused on what was happening in me that I couldn't love those around me. He wanted me afraid of myself. Fear has no eyes to see love.

And our flesh always focuses on how it looks. In my case, I wanted to be acceptable and pleasing to others. It's hard to listen to others when your mind-babble keeps thinking about self and self-performance.

Where would this thought lead me in five, ten, or thirty years if left unchecked? It would lead me to striving in everything I do. It would leave me believing I was a product of what people think of me more than who God says I am. It would leave me feeling unloved and unseen. That may lead to depression or to numbing techniques because of loneliness. It may also lead me to become super competitive with other women, and therefore judge and push away relationships. *Surely, I don't want this. Something must change. I must start to do a new thing.*

START

1. Submit to the Mind of Christ

To rehab and renew my heart, I begin with adoration for the lordship of Jesus. I adore the King by praying:

Jesus, You are more than enough. You are more than enough for my every need. You are all I need. You have all peace and all love in Your hands. You are the Prince of Peace. You are the Lord of Lords. You are my Lord. I submit to You in every way. I acknowledge You as the Author, Source, and Finisher of every good thing in my life. I lay down my ways for Yours. I agree with Your lordship and how You see me.

I also *renew my mind in the Word of God.* We talked about how the devil tempted Jesus. This is a good study to go into at this point. I also think about when Peter took a sword and struck the right ear off the high priest's servant coming at Jesus (John 18:10). Peter was quick to move! Quick to prove his allegiance. But he didn't have to defend Jesus. Jesus was more able to defend Himself than Peter ever could be.

God can always defend Himself. He doesn't need me to prove Him or protect Him; He wants me to rest in Him. "Neither height nor depth, nor anything else in all creation, will be able to separate us from the love of God that is in Christ Jesus our Lord" (Rom. 8:39).

If I am already loved, what is left to prove? If I am already in Christ, what can move me out of Him? I am secure and significant in His being.

At this point, I may write down on a note card or another piece of paper truths from Scripture, such as:

I am holy.
I am chosen.

I am loved, and nothing can separate me from God's love.
I am God's masterpiece.

Beyond this, here is what I am able to understand after praying and hearing what's on God's heart: *I can never prove enough.* The devil always leaves us with more to prove. It is an endless pursuit. At some point, if we are wise, we throw up our hands and say, "All this perfection business is futile."

Another declaration I can add to my list is: "The idea that I can reach some sort of nirvana or earthly perfection is a demonic delusion."

That will serve as a good reminder to me in the future.

I now use these declarations and speak them out loud over myself. The more I speak, the more my mind creates new neural pathways. I address not only the thought but also its underlying belief through these declarations.

2. Discover Any Unlocked Doors

What may have opened me up to this performance mindset? The first thing that comes to me is *fear.*

What door did I leave unlocked now or in my past?

I remember being a young girl, standing in front of my third-grade class, preparing to do show-and-tell. I wanted to tell my eager classmates about the blowtorch I saw doing street work in front of my house, but when I mentioned the word *fire,* everyone got excited.

"Did your house catch on fire?" they asked.

"Yes, it did," I answered.

Why did I lie? Because I finally felt like I—the odd girl out, the girl who sat on the sidewalk during recess—was getting the love and attention I'd so desperately craved and wanted. This was my moment to shine!

155

I learned: *You have to perform to be loved. And when you do, you get what your heart needs.*

This situation unlocked in me the intrusive thought that *I should perform to be loved.* It made me wonder, *What else can I do to gain attention and affirmation?*

It made me crave applause. People finally liked me.

Now, rather than leaving that door unlocked, I think upon this: *I don't live for other people's approval; I live from God's approval.* Whenever I start to think of what others are thinking about me, I turn my mind in a new direction. I consider what God may think about my heart, my prayers, and the direction of my life. I remember there is a cloud of witnesses in heaven cheering me on. I set my mind on heavenly things.

3. Repent, Renounce, and Pray

Father, I repent of trying to prove my worth. I repent of lying when I was a child. I repent of using what I do to cover the fear of who I am. I repent of not looking to You and Your Word to decide who I am. I break the agreement that I have to perform to be loved. I renounce any sort of need to compete, desire to be more than I am, stress to perform, or deception that I use to meet others' needs. Forgive me. I want no part in this demonic scheme. I come out of agreement with this, because nothing can separate me from Your love. If I am already in Your love, what else am I searching for? Thank You for forgiving me. In Jesus's name. Amen.

4. Go a New Way

The old way was stress and panic.
The new way is rest.

Let us therefore be zealous and exert ourselves and **strive diligently to enter that rest [of God, to know and experience it for ourselves],** that no one may fall or perish by the same kind of unbelief and disobedience [into which those in the wilderness fell]. (Heb. 4:11 AMPC)

Rather than working to gain love, I can rest in love. Notice here that rest is knowing and experiencing God. The more I know how God sees me and knows me, the more proving and striving fade into the background.

Practically, I can rest by:

- Asking God to help me to do the work He has for me, without leaving Him out.
- Understanding what pleases God and making that my chief aim.
- Remembering that I work from God's love, not for it.

5. Keep the Temple Shining

My wisest move here is to pray for future protection from this thought. Praying keeps us from disengaging from God.

"Now [Jesus] was telling them a parable to show that at all times they ought to pray and not become discouraged" (Luke 18:1 NASB). If Jesus thinks we ought to keep praying, we ought to keep praying. This is how we stay vigilant and on guard. This is how we, above all else, guard our hearts. This is how we don't lose heart.

Beyond this, I focus on what is good. I choose to go forward pleasing God more than pleasing other people. I keep Him as my main focus, and as I do, I trust that God will keep me in perfect peace. His Word says, "You keep him in perfect peace whose mind is stayed on you, because he trusts in you" (Isa. 26:3 ESV).

I pick up the sword of the Spirit, the Word of God, which continually reminds me of what is true. Having people around me with whom I can share is key. Remember, the heart can't always see itself. It is smart to have honest people around who know your heart and encourage you to a higher place.

They may say something to you like, "The reason why you're enough is because Christ is enough and He is in you." Or, "His power is perfected in your weakness." Or you may hear, "The story is not about your agony but His forthcoming glory."

The body of Christ is the hands and feet of Jesus. Do not block yourself from His body, from His caring and loving hands, because people have hurt you in the past. We need not only the headship of Christ but the body of Christ too. This is part of going a new way.

At another morning event I put on, my friends came around me and essentially said, "Kelly, the pressure is off of you." I was able to take a deep breath and just enjoy myself. I went a new way. God showed up.

12

Break Down the Lie of "I Shoulda, Woulda, or Coulda"

Failure is only the opportunity more intelligently to begin again.

Henry Ford, *My Life and Work*

I shoulda married that person.

I shoulda taken that job.

I shoulda spoken up.

I shoulda thought more about the situation.

I woulda been smarter had I applied myself.

I woulda been a better mom if I'd been nicer.

I woulda been more desirable if I hadn't gotten fat.

I woulda been less alone if I hadn't done that.

I coulda thought more before I talked.

I coulda acted different and that wouldn't have happened.

I coulda had a good marriage if only I didn't ___.

I coulda done a better job and everything would have been different.

Applying the Stop/Start Process

The lie we are going to address is: *If only I did ___; I messed everything up.*

More than three years ago, I was absolutely 100 percent not a good friend to someone. I still think about it. Rather than sharing my heart and having needed conversations, I excommunicated a friend. Frankly, like a runaway bride, I loudly announced to the person, "We're done."

I was afraid to speak truth to them. I was afraid to talk things out. So, I went cold turkey on the person by running away. They were shocked. I know it surprised them. They pretty much stopped talking to me (because I guess that is what I communicated that I wanted).

And I have struggled with that moment again and again and again. *Why did I act like that? Why couldn't I have handled things better?*

Despite my later efforts to make amends and apologize, I have no relationship with that person now. I wish I could go back. A couple of days ago, I visited the person's Facebook page and many of those old feelings washed over me again.

If only I could go back; I messed everything up.

My face fell. My eyes looked down. I felt horribly sad. Then I clicked out of the page. I tried to pretend everything was okay. I hated myself for doing what I did. I couldn't fix it. The moment was done, but the pain was still there.

Let's begin to work out the two-part Stop/Start Process as it pertains to my thought.

STOP

1. Capture the Thought

I realized I felt sad, discouraged, and disappointed in myself when I saw that friend's Facebook page. My thoughts were: *I want to go back in time. I messed everything up.* The underlying belief was: *I did badly. I am bad. My future won't be good because of this.*

2. Determine Who Is Speaking

Is this God speaking to me? One thing I know is—after repentance—God doesn't look back. He says what is forgiven is done. He also says my sins are removed "as far as the east is from the west" (Ps. 103:12) and He remembers them no more. Clearly, I know by the Word of God that the thoughts in my head are not the thoughts of the mind of Christ.

But is it the devil speaking to me? Accusation post-repentance is the enemy. If God forgave us and we are still accused, the accuser is speaking.

Beyond this, who else may be speaking? Is my flesh talking? This Scripture gives us some insight:

> Now the works of the flesh are evident: sexual immorality, impurity, sensuality, idolatry, sorcery, enmity, strife, jealousy, fits of anger, rivalries, dissensions, divisions, envy, drunkenness, orgies, and things like these. (Gal. 5:19–21 ESV)

It does not appear that this thought is speaking predominantly from my flesh, which confirms that it is more likely a thought from the accuser.

3. Understand Intent

Where did the enemy intend to take me with this thought? The devil wants me to believe I'll never be a good friend again.

Why bother? I'll hurt people. I am awkward. He also tells me that everyone knows how foolishly I acted in this situation. He insists that I am on a blacklist and should be embarrassed.

Ultimately, be it five, ten, or thirty years down the road, I believe he aims to make me feel like a bad Christian. He wants me to think that I am no good and God doesn't want me anymore. He wants me to figure, based on how my friend doesn't talk to me anymore, that God doesn't talk to me either. He hopes I'll give up on my Christian walk, isolate myself, and turn in. I'll hang out in my basement and not come out. I'll hate myself and think everyone else does too. Who knows? I may even want to give up on life.

Seeing this makes me realize I have to fight the devil, because he surely is fighting to take me down. To be complacent about this fight would be to lose the battle in the long run.

START

1. Submit to the Mind of Christ

First, I adore the King by praying:

Father God, I thank You that You are ever-forgiving. You are merciful, slow to anger, and abounding in steadfast love. You are so giving that You would give Your only Son for me. You are the giver of good things. You are faithful, even when I am not. You are amazing. Your Son is the best gift of my life. He saved me, and He still saves. His blood is enough. His blood covers all of me, even the worst of me. I receive the blood and give it total ownership of my life. I submit to the mind of Christ and give it total ownership in all I do. You are greater than me. Bigger than me. More able to cover me than me. In Jesus's name. Amen.

Turning, then, to renew my mind with the Word of God, I agree with Paul's sentiment, "But one thing I do: Forgetting what is behind and straining toward what is ahead, I press on toward the goal" (Phil. 3:13–14). I apply it to my life.

I will never get ahead by looking back. Putting the car in reverse never sends it forward.

Jesus declared, "No one who puts a hand to the plow and looks back is fit for service in the kingdom of God" (Luke 9:62). The kingdom of God is made for people who are moving into something new, not for people who dwell in the old.

"And God is able to bless you abundantly, so that in all things at all times, having all that you need, you will abound in every good work" (2 Cor. 9:8). God has all I need to walk into good new things. His grace is ready for me. I am not left feeling it was all for naught. I am not bad. I am still good in God's eyes.

Therefore, I make a declaration sheet that says:

I am loved.

I forget what lies behind for the better gain of Christ Jesus that is ahead.

I do not look back, for I trust God in what is coming.

I didn't miss it. I am right in God's grace, and it is abounding toward me.

I release my friend, and I bless them in all their ways.

2. Discover Any Unlocked Doors

What may have left the door unlocked and opened me to feeling this way? What boundary did I let down? What responsibility do I need to take going forward? What is under my thoughts? Is there something from my history that I need to repent of?

In this case, I did not accept forgiveness. This can be a big error. If we don't receive forgiveness, we will continually receive shame and accusation.

I kept looking back and feeling bad. I had an unlocked door because, clearly, I did not think Christ's grace was enough to cover my mistake—or else I would have received it. Instead, I kept ruminating on what I had done wrong. I opened the door to dwelling on those thoughts by dwelling too long on that old friend's Facebook page. I could have avoided that pity party altogether.

Indeed, there is a time for sorrow, but if the sorrow continues for a decade, at some point there is a clear reason to move on.

3. Repent, Renounce, and Pray

Father, I repent. I repent of not trusting that the work Christ did is enough for the likes of me. I repent of looking back and thinking I missed out. Your grace is redeeming grace. I break the agreement that Your grace is not enough, that I have permanently missed out, and that I ruin things. You can redeem and renew all things, even me. I trust Your redeeming work, even if it happens with a new friend. I repent of putting my opinions above Your truth, the Word of God. Bring me great relationships. Restore what the enemy has stolen. In Jesus's name. Amen.

4. Go a New Way

This verse pops out at me: "But forget all that—it is nothing compared to what I am going to do" (Isa. 43:18 NLT). This was true for the Israelites in the original context of that verse and is equally true for us today. God is always doing a new thing. That is what His grace is. Grace is the empowerment, enablement, and equipping of a new thing!

Grace is independent of our action—or inaction—and wholly dependent on Jesus's action on the cross. With grace, what was not can be. The glory of this new thing can even surpass the weight of the old loss.

Thinking along these lines encourages a heart to go a new way—a faith-filled way that leans on trust and Christ's finished work that always leads forward.

5. Keep the Temple Shining

Here, rather than dwelling on what I didn't do, I pray for new relationships. I move on them when I see God opening the door. I open my spirit up to receive from the Holy Spirit each new day.

Then I think on what is good. This requires me to not go back to the dog dung. This means I do not go looking back at that friend's Facebook page. I can pray a blessing over them, when I think of them, but I don't track back.

Beyond this, I use the sword of the Spirit—my declarations—going forward, and I raise up my shield of faith to keep enemy arrows at bay. I say:

God does have goodness and mercy for me in the land of the living.
God does have a hope and a future for me, despite me.
I am a good friend by the grace of God; He will help me.
In this, I can have the courage of heart and mind to carry on.

For it is [not your strength, but it is] God who is effectively at work in you, both to will and to work [that is, strengthening, energizing, and creating in you the longing and the ability to fulfill your purpose] for His good pleasure. (Phil. 2:13 AMP)

13

Break Down the Lie of "I'm Not Wanted, I'm Lonely and Rejected"

What lies behind us and what lies before us are tiny matters compared to what lies within us.

Henry S. Haskins, *Meditations in Wall Street*

Kelly, this picture is for the friends who got here first, not for you. Could you stand aside while we take the picture—just us?"

All the other women at the party, pretty in their party best as they stood next to beautiful displays of fruit, yummy foods, and pink ornaments, just stared at me. The air hung dead and silent. Everyone knew: Kelly needed to move aside.

I was embarrassed.

What would I do now? I hadn't the faintest idea. Frankly, I was frozen for a moment, taken off guard, not sure what to say. On top of that, I'd already suffered one rejection when I first walked into this party, as one person whom I considered a friend didn't even greet me when I arrived. She ignored me and kept talking to the picture-taker, the lady who wanted me gone. Was it because she was pleasing her friend?

One could assume . . . and certainly I did.

So much inside of me wanted to hate. The woman who asked me to leave the picture had been standoffish and distant to me in the past. Her move seemed passive-aggressive. Plus, how did that logic work—you're more worthy if you're early and helpful? Or maybe just if you're *in the club*?

I wanted nothing to do with this club. I wanted to hide behind the plastic tablecloth that held the impeccably pretty, ornate displays of sandwiches and treats—or maybe I could make a quick escape. Being anywhere but there would be fine, really.

This picture-perfect moment was *for them* and *not for me*.

The women started to assemble, taking their positions for the picture, all fashionable and pretty and cute, carefully staggering themselves. I remained frozen off to the side, hoping to quietly fall into the swimming pool unnoticed. Maybe I'd transport to an unseen place called Quiet Nothingville, or perhaps Not-Here Town, USA. Instead, I just held my gut tight and, with all my might, kept my emotions in.

That is until my thoughts were interrupted as a voice spoke up from the crowd, like an angel. An older woman said, "Kelly, get in here!"

And I could move again. Breathe again. Her words brought wind to my chest.

My head and heart wanted to rest on her comforting shoulder. I wanted to cry it out with this woman. I wanted to let her know how amazing and kind and generous and wonderful she was, and how nonexclusive and noncliquey she was being. How much of a safe refuge she was in the midst of this club. But I didn't. I only pondered these things in my heart and gave silent thanks for her.

168

I still think about her. I've forgiven the picture-taking woman and the friend who ignored me. Somehow I know that they have no clue how they hurt me. Plus, I've hurt people too—and not even realized it. And, more recently, I've watched this lady change her approach; I've noticed, and I appreciate it.

But that doesn't take away how I felt in the moment. Have you ever felt rejected or abandoned to some degree? Perhaps you've thought:

I'm not wanted.

I'm lonely.

No one likes me.

I am always unchosen.

I am always hurt.

People don't think of me.

People don't appreciate me.

I am not important.

I don't fit in.

They must think I am inferior.

No one sees me.

I feel sorry for myself.

Applying the Stop/Start Process

The lie we are going to address is: *I am not wanted*. This thought pattern may be more easily understood by analyzing a situation that happened to me.

One day I informed my husband, "I want a date night." I imagined the perfect night would be free of distractions and deterrents so we could fully connect with each other.

My husband nodded and carried on with his day.

A few hours later, without mentioning anything about our date, he got back to me and said, "I scheduled a business dinner for you and me with a businesswoman and her husband whom I want you to meet."

He did *what*? What had happened to *our* date night? The one where we connect and have great conversation and look in each other's eyes?

Who comes first—me or the business? Didn't I just tell him I needed a date?

Once again, I felt rejected. I had put myself on the line and now I was being left behind: *You're not wanted, Kelly!*

I let him know I was upset. He should put me first. I wanted *my* date night. I mattered!

My husband agreed that I mattered. He agreed to set up a second date night because I was important.

A week passed.

I brought up the date night again.

He said okay. The date night still didn't happen.

I told him a couple of days later, "Maybe we can do dinner tonight."

He said, "Eh . . ."

Later that day he told me, "I scheduled us a lunch/work meeting with another couple."

What? This was happening a second time?

He's rejecting me. Why does this keep happening?

Let's begin to work out the two-part Stop/Start Process as it pertains to my thought.

STOP

1. Capture the Thought

I felt abandoned, rejected, hurt, and lonely. My thoughts were: *I'm being rejected. People don't like me. They don't want to be with me.* My belief underneath was: *Maybe I am not good enough. Maybe I am flawed.*

2. Determine Who Is Speaking

Could these thoughts about being flawed be from God? Most certainly not! They are killing my identity. They are destroying my sense of self. They are stealing hope. They are speaking lies about my husband, who loves me very much.

Those are sure signs the enemy is involved. Also involved is my flesh, as we'll come to see. Whenever our world circles on the axis of *self*, that's a sign our flesh may be speaking. This was certainly happening for me.

3. Understand Intent

What was behind the enemy's scheme to reject me? To isolate me. Where would I be five, ten, or thirty years down the road with this thought growing larger and larger in my mind? Likely I would have pushed all people away. I would be by myself and full of fear. I would probably also be a very sad and depressed individual. I am not sure others would want to be around me.

START

1. Submit to the Mind of Christ

I adore the King by praying:

Father, thank You that Jesus is my Lord. Jesus is my King. I don't submit to how people look, feel, or act toward me; I look to You. You have made my life. I am significant in Your eyes. How You see me is how I choose to see me. I submit to Your leadership and Your words about me, and I welcome the kingship of Jesus in my life. I want to rely on Jesus more than people. I want to rely on Christ in me more

than my own sense of self. God, You are faithful. I am Your
daughter. I am loved. I am chosen. I am holy in Your sight.
In Jesus's name. Amen.

I then renew my mind with the Word of God:

Furthermore, because we are united with Christ, we have received
an inheritance from God, for he chose us in advance, and he makes
everything work out according to his plan.

God decided in advance to adopt us into his own family by
bringing us to himself through Jesus Christ. This is what he wanted
to do, and it gave him great pleasure. (Eph. 1:11, 5 NLT)

I ask the Holy Spirit, submitting myself to the mind of Christ,
to reveal anything about how wanted I am, loved I am, and chosen
I am. I am reminded of how I have been freed by grace. "So if the
Son sets you free, you will be free indeed" (John 8:36).

If Jesus set me free of the yoke of being tied up to other people's
responses, why do I keep tying myself up again?

From all this, I write declarations to speak over myself daily,
which include:

Christ has chosen to live inside of me. He wants me.

All things will work out according to Christ's plan—I don't
have to fear how it looks.

Even when I feel alone or left behind, I am united with
Christ.

God has good plans for me and good relationships for me.

I am adopted into Christ's family, and I belong.

2. Discover Any Unlocked Doors

How did this intruding thought—*I am not wanted*—get in?
The first thing that strikes me is one word: *sensitivity*. Likely, my

husband was not trying to hurt me. Neither was that woman at the party. The truth is, I can sometimes take things personally. My unlocked door is making things about myself when they largely aren't. What opened me up to feeling sensitive and taking things personally? A self-focus.

When I operate with a God-focus, however, it is not about what I feel entitled to and what I am getting but rather how I am giving and how I am loving. When I return to me-centered thoughts, I lose God-centered thoughts. I cut my connection with the mind of Christ.

3. Repent, Renounce, and Pray

Father God, I repent of being sensitive and taking things personally. Help me keep my eyes more on You than on what other people do. I break the agreement that people will always reject me or hurt me. I break the agreement that You won't protect me. I also receive the truth that You have great relationships for me. I renounce strong and bitter responses and repent of them. Help me not to accuse my brother or sister but to love them. Give me grace to live out love and not judgment. In Jesus's name. Amen.

4. Go a New Way

Galatians 5:1 says, "It is for freedom that Christ has set us free. Stand firm, then, and do not be encumbered once more by a yoke of slavery" (BSB).

We are not unwanted; we are more wanted than we could ever know or understand. If Christ is in us, doesn't that prove He wants us? This is the ground we stand on and return to.

We have to stand firm!

If a person can steal our footing on Christ Jesus, our footing was not strong enough to begin with!

With the solid rock reestablished as our firm footing, we now can:

- Choose friends we like and trust—people who communicate in a straightforward way.
- Keep our minds in the light, as Christ is in the light, instead of allowing our thoughts to go to dark places of assumptions and presumptions.
- Ask questions and seek to understand where others are coming from.
- Give people the benefit of the doubt.
- Put ourselves out there to meet new people and risk trusting others.
- Expect to connect, rather than the opposite.
- Carry peace, while not trying to be anything more than God created us to be.

Why? Because no matter how much or how little other people seem to want us, we know God always does.

5. Keep the Temple Shining

I pray for future protection from this thought, saying something like:

Thank You, God, that Your Word says, "Nothing can ever separate [me] from God's love. Neither death nor life, neither angels nor demons, neither [my] fears for today nor [my] worries about tomorrow—not even the powers of hell can separate [me] from God's love. No power in the sky above or in the earth below—indeed, nothing in all creation will ever be able to separate [me] from the love of God that is revealed in Christ Jesus our Lord" (Rom. 8:38–39 NLT). Your love is inescapable, inconceivable, and infinite. I cannot walk out of it. I can't reach the end of it. It is near to me. It is available. I walk in it. I talk in it, even if I can't understand the depths of it. I trust You. I know that You will protect me and keep me. I can trust You in my relationships. You will help me, even when my feelings are hurt. You are the ultimate Counselor. Help me to believe You over what people do to me. In Jesus's name. Amen.

To think about what is good in this situation, I open my aperture to let more light in, as if using a camera. With more light, I can get a clearer and crisper picture about what is really happening. Here, I can see: my husband is kind and caring 99 percent of the time. He loves to spend time with me. He is giving and generous. To think on what is good is to recognize that this date night issue was 0.001 percent of my marriage and not a declaration on my whole future. It was just a moment. Moments happen; life goes on. An open aperture helps put things into perspective.

To grab my sword of the Spirit, in this case, is to remember Jesus. Or, more specifically, John 1:11, "He came to that which was his own, but his own did not receive him."

Jesus came in the fullness of every gift, every amount of goodness, every good intention, and every blessing, yet *His own people* didn't receive Him. If Jesus wasn't received, what in the world makes me believe I'll be received by everyone? That's an unrealistic expectation. And it's not biblical. I have to deal with the fact that not everyone will like me, want me, or jibe with me. So what? If Jesus was rejected, I can draw on His empathy, His story, and His Spirit when I also am rejected. To be rejected by others is never to remain unwanted. Jesus always wants me, and He also is able to sympathize and empathize with my feelings and weaknesses.

Now, in order to pick up the shield of faith, I consider someone who may have lost faith, such as Peter. He rejected Jesus three times. And yet Jesus restored him three times, saying, "Feed my sheep" (John 21:17).

It's almost like He was saying to Peter, "You may have thought I rejected you, but I still want you and love you no matter what." Think about what is good, and remember:

You are not abandoned; you are kept.

You are not walking alone; the Spirit of God is always in you.

You are not left behind; the very mind of Christ is in you.

You are not who you seem to be; you are who God declares you to be.

You are not who others demand you be; you are who God says you are.

Today is a fresh day with fresh mercies, and we are all new creations!

But you are a chosen race, a royal priesthood, a dedicated nation, [God's] own **purchased**, special people, **that you may set forth the wonderful deeds and display the virtues and perfections of Him** Who called you out of darkness into His marvelous light. (1 Pet. 2:9 AMPC)

When I know the power of the light inside of me, my mind is illuminated by Truth itself—and I can't help but shine, no matter what!

14

Break Down the Lie of "I Can't Really Trust God"

Have faith that there is such a great inheritance of love that no matter how far you travel away, there are enough love excesses and deep reserves to take you all the way back home.

Approximately a decade ago, I kept waking up in the night in torment. I'd snap awake from deep sleep and ask myself, *Am I saved? What if I am not really saved? Can I really trust God to save me?*

I would go through every detail of how I'd accepted Jesus—what I said and how my heart was—and I'd stay up for hours doing this.

I confessed that Jesus was my Lord and Savior while I was in my bedroom. I didn't do it in front of people. Was that enough? Surely, I have stood up for Jesus in front of others by now.

Do I have enough fruit? I think I do.

What if I don't do everything just right? Will Jesus still want me?

Doubt is having a double mind. It sends our minds in two directions. Rather than relying on the mind of Christ, by the Holy Spirit, we revert back to the thoughts of the flesh.

Do you experience double-mindedness?

Do you ever say to yourself, *I think that's what I should do, but should I really? God is calling me to do ___, but do I really have time to do ___?*

I am going to quit eating junk food, but this brownie is okay for today. Should I send this email or not (time passes, and it is never sent)? Should I offer to help, or maybe I shouldn't?

Double-mindedness is delay that makes room for us to disobey.

Perhaps you've had these thoughts:

I'm not sure—I can't decide.

I doubt my decision, and I wish I'd done something else.

Maybe I'm wrong.

I don't know what to do.

I have to put off this decision because I don't know.

I need to give in and do it how people want me to.

I want to say no, but I am going to say yes.

Applying the Stop/Start Process

The lie we are going to address is: *Can I really trust God to ___?* As in, *Can I really trust God to save me?*

We either trust God or not. There is no gray area.

Will God save, or is He not Savior anymore?

Will God really come through, or is He not in that business any longer?

Will God really do as He says He will, or is He done being true to His Word?

Will He really help, or is the Holy Spirit not the Helper like
the Word says He is (John 14:16)?
Will God be true to His nature?

Recently I reread part of this book and hated it. I thought every
word was bland and boring. Every point seemed unimportant and
dull. The sentences didn't pop. The flow was off. Apprehension
started up in me like a tension headache that wouldn't let go.

But then I felt God stop me in my tracks, raising questions.
Would I trust Him or not? Would I lean on His Word more than
mine, or would I question everything? Would I walk by faith and
not by sight, or would I doubt?

Whose word would I choose to lean on?

In this space, I remembered that I don't rely on my power; I
rely on God's. I remembered how Paul did not come with lofty or
eloquent speech but resolved to know nothing but Christ crucified
(1 Cor. 2:2). I remembered how Jesus compared those who seek
glory for themselves against those who want to honor God, saying,
"Those who speak for themselves want glory only for themselves,
but a person who seeks to honor the one who sent him speaks
truth, not lies" (John 7:18 NLT).

I know what camp I want to be in. I want to trust Him and
honor Him, despite me. The only option here is to trust God at
His Word. *It's not my words that save but His. It is not my words
that are fruitful but His.*

> It is the same with my word.
> I send it out, and it always produces fruit.
> It will accomplish all I want it to,
> and it will prosper everywhere I send it.
> (Isa. 55:11 NLT)

His Word is His mind to help us. His Word advances and
prospers us. After realizing this, I took my thoughts captive and

recaptured the mind of Christ. *I move out so God's power can move in!*

This is a biblical principle all of us should hold tightly to. When we move out of the way, Christ's power moves in.

It doesn't matter how we feel; it matters who He is and what He says. It doesn't matter what we think of our work; it matters how He wants to work. And our doubt doesn't matter either; what matters is His power ready to work through us, His submitted vessels.

> But he said to me, "My grace is sufficient for you, for my power is made perfect in weakness." Therefore I will boast all the more gladly about my weaknesses, so that Christ's power may rest on me. (2 Cor. 12:9)

As we honor the Father, Jesus releases the power. This power accomplishes the Father's will, ushers in the kingdom of God, and gives us "all these things" we tend to worry about, as His Word says: "But seek first his kingdom and his righteousness, and all these things will be given to you as well" (Matt. 6:33).

When we trust, we let go of our own minds to be led by the mind of Christ. Trust turns submitted vessels into more than conquerors through the ever-working power of the Son. Trust seeks His way more than its own. Trust leans heavily on the words "His grace is enough" and returns to this truth often.

Then it follows Jesus no matter where He goes or what the cost. How can trust do all this? Trust thoughtfully discerns what God would have it to do (Eph. 5:17–19). Even more, it miraculously knows and finds the will of God, because its transformed nature is filled with the mind of Christ. "Let God transform you into a new person by changing the way you think. *Then you will learn to know God's will for you*, which is good and pleasing and perfect" (Rom. 12:2 NLT).

Even Jesus needed to seek and trust the Father's will. He said, "Father, if you are willing, take this cup from me; yet not my will, but yours be done" (Luke 22:42). Then Jesus had the right mind to follow through on the Father's mission. With a single mind and a single eye on the joy set before Him, Jesus died on the cross, honoring the Father's plan with all His body and redeeming us with all His blood.

Step 1: Stop

1. Capture the Thought

Let's get practical as we work through the process of starting and stopping.

When I doubted my work in this book, I was feeling overwhelmed and nervous. I wanted to throw my work in the trash because my heart thumped with the worry that everything would not be okay.

My underlying beliefs were: *I am going to be embarrassed if this book is horrible. I fear that if I trust God, things still will not turn out okay. I am going to get hurt. God will not rescue me. I may find out God is not real, and everything will be ruined. Therefore, I have to put up a wall and protect myself from all these horrible feelings by controlling, manipulating, or doing things on my own. I have to trash my work before I get hurt by any of these things.*

2. Determine Who Is Speaking

Here, I have to ask myself: Who is speaking? God? The devil? Or my flesh?

Certainly, thoughts of doubt are not from God.

So, are they from the devil? Remember, he asked Eve, "Did God really say, 'You must not eat from any tree in the garden'?" (Gen. 3:1). That's a doubt-raising sort of question, isn't it?

Doubt can certainly be a demonic attack. But, in this case, it wasn't only the devil in charge of my behavior. I had to take responsibility for some of it too. My flesh didn't want to be embarrassed.

I was fearing others' responses and what they would think of my work.

Honesty is the best policy for getting rid of tormenting thoughts. Only after being brutally honest about our responsibility in sin can we be freed of it.

What may you need to be brutally honest about? Is there any sin that you have been deflecting on the enemy that you may need to take responsibility for?

Remember, it is the truth that sets us free.

3. Understand Intent

What purpose of God or fruit of the Spirit is the enemy trying to destroy? What is he trying to keep us from by launching this attack? These are the questions we should ask ourselves when understanding intent.

First, we should know the devil is a legalist. He wants to bind us to the law so we can't be freed by grace. Sometimes I have been guilty of using what I do for God as reason to justify why I am good. On the flip side, I also judge what I haven't done as a reason why God may not want me. These are human reasonings and arguments that we should demolish (2 Cor. 10:5), as they are apart from the grace of Jesus, which doesn't save us because of our own work. "For it is by grace you have been saved, through faith—and this is not from yourselves, it is the gift of God—not by works, so that no one can boast" (Eph. 2:8–9).

We don't stand on what we do for God; we stand on what Jesus has done for us. Sometimes I get these two mixed up. These are subtleties the enemy uses to entangle. The devil wants us propped up and looking religious but with no real power, no radical reliance on Jesus that releases strength despite our weakness. The Bible, explaining the end times, says, "They will act religious, but they will reject the power that could make them godly. Stay away from people like that!" (2 Tim. 3:5 NLT).

Where does the devil want us to be five, ten, or thirty years down the road as we continue down this path? Like Adam and Eve, who fell into doubt, the devil wants to lead us to shame, to separation from the presence of God, and to a life where we run away from God rather than toward Him. He wants that small seed of doubt to grow huge. For then we will be unstable in all our ways. "A double-minded man [is] unstable in all his ways" (James 1:8 ESV).

Yet we can say no to these schemes by saying yes to Jesus and to His mind that wants to help us go another way.

START

1. Submit to the Mind of Christ

First, I adore the King by praying:

Father, You are the God of all creation. You know what You are doing. You know all things. You have all power. You are in charge. Your ways are right. You do not question or doubt Your own plan. Why? Because You are the Source of all life. The Maker. The Creator. In You we live and move and have our being. All Your ways are right. All Your truth is right. All Your truth is good. You make good decisions as pertains to my life. Today, I come to You and submit my whole self to You. I let go of everything for the better gain of trusting You. Lead me in all Your ways. May the mind of Christ be prominent over any thoughts of doubt I may have so I can stay close to You and Your love. In Jesus's name. Amen.

The Word of God renews our minds, and the mind of Christ eases doubt. All the time, I hear that still, small whisper, *Trust Me, Kelly.* I answer back, "I do, God. I trust You."

But do I?

Trust in the LORD with **all your heart**
and lean not on your own understanding;
in all your ways submit to him,
and he will **make your paths straight**. (Prov. 3:5–6)

Trust—despite our own opinions, summations, and past experiences—is the quickest and most direct path to destinations of God. With it, we bypass many layovers. Double-mindedness only brings us delays, stops, and stalls.

For instance, when I sought God by discerning His heart, as I described at the start of this chapter, I moved beyond my own understanding and into His will. He reminded me of the power of His Word to transform. As a result, I was reinvigorated and restored by the idea that it was His Word that would save, not my writing. I didn't have to run in circles of worry about my own words anymore.

The process of understanding through the mind of Christ, via the Holy Spirit, is vitally important. I've learned over time that even one word from the mind of Christ, founded on the Word of God, has the power to save us from thoughts of doubt and torment nearly every time. Here, we can't help but gain faith.

Faith defeats double-mindedness. Faith also pleases God.

"It is impossible to please God without faith" (Heb. 11:6 NLT). Do you have faith? Have you sought God for faith when plagued by thoughts of doubt? My friend, faith does not rely on what it sees but on what God says. Faith does not look at what cannot be but trusts that "everything is possible for one who believes" (Mark 9:23).

Faith reaches far beyond the natural constructs of our own understanding, arguments, and theories. It transcends worry. It guts fear. "The righteous will live by faith" (Gal. 3:11).

This is not the hour to shrink back; faith presses in and goes out to reach people, cities, nations, and the world for Jesus. "But my righteous one will live by faith. And I take no pleasure in the one who shrinks back" (Heb. 10:38).

Faith is a gift from God (Eph. 2:8). The Giver gives it; we receive it and act on it. To be one with the mind of Christ is to be one with His Word, His truth, and His will. For me? To prepare my mind, I remind my soul how I can trust the Lord.

My straight path is found by trusting God and His Word.

I live by faith and not by sight. God's Word is the final authority.

God is greater than my doubt. He will free me.

I please God when I don't waver but believe Him.

I don't lean on what I understand but trust God with all my heart. He will take me where I need to go.

God is faithful to His Word to perform it.

"God is not human, that he should lie" (Num. 23:19); He is worthy of all my trust.

2. Discover Any Unlocked Doors

How did I get myself in this place of doubt? Did something set me off? Is there something from my past that I need to handle? Is fear behind this? Did a person or a situation provoke this?

Frankly, sometimes my past makes me doubt God for my future. Even though I've gone through a lot, I have to acknowledge a few things. There have been times when God hasn't given me all I wanted—but He always gave me all I needed. There are times when I'm quite certain I didn't get an earthly reward because He was setting me up for a better return—a heavenly reward. Many times I didn't get the go-ahead because I believe He was working out the perfect timing.

Even when the "I still haven't seen it" moments feel hard, the hard truth is *God is still working.* He is still working things out. He is still pulling strings in the right order so the entire show of

His glory works out for good. The whole story is not just about me. There are other people, circumstances, and life scenarios God is weaving and working out for the complete fulfillment of His ultimate glory.

Will we be okay with what God is still working out? With what He is weaving for His glory, even if we have to wait?

I don't like to wait. I like my coffee fast. I like an answer quickly. I don't like traffic. I hate struggling. Wildernesses? No thank you.

> Now to him who is able to do **immeasurably more than all we ask or imagine,** according to his power that is at work within us, to him be glory in the church and in Christ Jesus throughout all generations, for ever and ever! Amen. (Eph. 3:20–21)

3. Repent, Renounce, and Pray

Father, forgive me. You say a double-minded person is unstable in all their ways. I no longer want to be double-minded. You also say they should not expect to get what they ask for. I ask You to forgive me for doubting. When the enemy comes, let me be quick to say no to doubt. Let me come to You first, before I turn to my own ruminating thoughts. Your mind is not my mind. Your thoughts are not my thoughts. I need You. I break the agreement that all my thinking and postulating can come to a better conclusion than Your Word. I break the agreement that worry works to produce something. It produces nothing but endless run-around-the-track lack of progress. Forgive me. I want to live in line with Your mind and not my own. In Jesus's name. Amen.

4. Go a New Way

> Blessed is the person who obeys the law of the LORD.
> They don't follow the advice of evil people.
> They don't make a habit of doing what sinners do.
> They don't join those who make fun of the LORD and
> his law.

Instead, the law of the LORD gives them joy.
They think about his law day and night.
(Ps. 1:1–2 NIrV)

We don't do what sinners do. Sinners doubt. They do not believe God. They rebel. They forget about love. They carry offense. They sin. This is not the lifestyle of a Jesus follower.

Our way is God's way. His Word is our mental word. His love becomes our love, as we are transformed into His image and likeness.

To go a new way is to release forgiveness to *all* those who have hurt us. It is to sit with God and to release past offenses. It is to ask Him how we can trust Him today. We let go of what hurt us yesterday for a better today. What might we need to let go of from our past? What disobedience or distrust has led our hearts and minds astray?

This morning, in the quiet hour when the sun was rising above my front porch, a place laden with mosquitoes, I asked God what people and what hurts I needed to forgive today. I did not expect to write a list of thirty-one things. Wow. Unforgiveness, bitterness, and resentment hide. Yet acknowledging and releasing these internal intruders is the key to complete trust.

How can we trust God when we have been hurt so much? When we carry so many injuries, traumas, and wounds? When we are burdened and pained? How can we follow Jesus when we are weighed down?

We can't. We must let go to receive. We must release what we hold to receive His *more*. We must abandon all the weight to walk like Jesus walked.

What or who might we need to forgive today? Our forgiving is how God goes about giving us something greater. God is *for-giving*. He gave His Son, for those willing to receive Him.

Forgiving is the process by which we open our hands to receive the better thing God is giving. As we unclench our fists, our hands become open and ready for what He wants to put in them.

This morning, as I forgave, I realized God was giving me greater freedom to be myself. Like two erasers being clapped together, He was removing the grimy chalk that had caked up on me. Why was this so important to going a new way? So I could trust God and the mind of Christ more in my daily life.

What does this look like practically in our lives as we trust God, others, and ourselves more?

> It looks like being fearless where we would have once been afraid people would judge us.
>
> It looks like being true to who we are no matter how the past demeaned us.
>
> It looks like having bold love despite others' reactions.
>
> It looks like picking up the calling we set down because we didn't believe God would really help us.
>
> It looks like being freed from self-torture and self-condemnation because Jesus's grace is bigger than any human frailty.
>
> It looks like moving ahead, in the face of fear, because we believe God is good and will help us.

5. Keep the Temple Shining

If I start to fall into doubt, mistrust, or fear, I return to God. I say something like:

Father, I thank You that You are in charge. You know what You are doing. I want to trust You more than anything I see or know. I ask You to guard my heart and mind in Christ Jesus. I ask for Your peace. I ask for faith so big that I stand firm and steadfast no matter what giant comes against me.

Please keep me from temptation. Help me remember Jesus.
He is worthy of all my trust. He trusted even when Your way
was a cross. I can trust too. I thank You that You are worthy
of all my trust. You are mighty to save. You are powerful.
Never once has someone trusted You wrongly. Every time,
You are faithful! In Jesus's name. Amen.

After praying this, I am reminded that even if I *feel* scared, I can *go forward* anyway.

When I know the right thing to do, I obey immediately. If attacks rise up, I don't let my mind go there. I think upon what is good. I remember all the ways in my life God has been faithful. I use "His faithful promises [as my] armor and protection" (Ps. 91:4 NLT).

God never breaks a promise. Knowing this protects me. My response to God remains consistent: "Here I am, God. Your servant is listening and willing. Whatever You want, Father. It's Your will be done and Your kingdom come."

My faith will defeat my double-mindedness. I am most powerful when I move quickly and decisively.

What about you? How will you encourage yourself? What will you speak if distrust, disobedience, or double-mindedness rise up in you?

I believe it is vital that we all remember what we hold. The sword of the Spirit, the Word of God, is not a toy sword but a powerful and effective weapon able to cut and pierce. This is important, because if we think we're playing with a flimsy plastic sword, we will move hesitantly and timidly. No. We do not hold a weak sword. Our sword is big. It is sharp. It is effective. It is powerful. Mighty.

We must remember the power we hold through God's Word and through the Holy Spirit. And we must use it. Our sword is meant to take back ground from the enemy. It is meant to move God's kingdom into a dying world.

When we trust God, we speak with boldness. "Whoever speaks *is to do so as one who is speaking actual words of God*" (1 Pet. 4:11 NASB). We speak believing God more than our own fear or our perceived reality. We speak with bold love for others. We speak grace over ourselves when we make mistakes. By the mind of Christ, we speak as one speaking the actual words of God.

When we speak, we speak Christ.

Aligned with His mind, we speak words that destroy doubt—and not only our personal doubt but the doubt of the world. Others hear Jesus through us and find His love.

This is what trust releases.

15

Break Down the Lie of "I Have to Do Something about This"

My deepest awareness of myself is that I am deeply loved by Jesus Christ and I have done nothing to earn or deserve it.

Brennan Manning, *The Ragamuffin Gospel*

Once upon a time, there was a soldier in the midst of a war. Enemy troops were approaching over the hill; he could see them from the cover of the bunker he and his fellow soldiers were in. Safe and undercover, the commander began to talk about the master plan, and the team listened intently, minds in the game—except one.

Without as much as a "go word" from his commander, the soldier got up and said, "I'm going to go out there, into the war, and I'll handle everything."

The commander looked concerned. This wasn't the plan, and it certainly wasn't a winning tactic, so he reminded the young soldier, "Son, you don't have to be the savior."

But the soldier said, "I want to be," and he launched himself from the safety of the bunker to charge the enemy line, guns blazing.

Thousands of troops moved toward him. Tanks came up over the horizon. Firing sounded everywhere. And this one lone ranger? This supposed savior of the whole war? He ran into the fray pridefully thinking he could handle it alone. It was over quickly. The warrior who ran alone was shot within three seconds.

Silence sat on the battlefield.

The commander turned to the remaining troops. "Now, will you all trust me? You don't always need to do something; you just need to trust me."

The remaining soldiers nodded.

Our attempts to fix things can kill us—and others. Our best attempts to win God's war, apart from Him, are fruitless.

I should know. I step in to handle things far more than letting God be my Commander. When my family is upset, I jump in to offer solutions quickly. When my husband has a hard day, I tell him how to fix his feelings. When people need me, I make myself available despite my own needs.

Like me, do you ever feel like you have to do it all and be it all? Maybe you've thought:

I need to figure things out.

I need to make my own way.

I have to hold things together.

I need to go faster.

I can't fail.

I need to handle this situation, or nobody else will.

I can't trust anyone.

I have to get everything done right now, before I can relax.

I need people to agree with me.

I am a savior.

Are there times you do more than what God is calling you to do? Do you intervene into lanes that aren't yours to travel in? Do you overexert yourself?

Applying the Stop/Start Process

The lie we are going to address is: *I have to step in and do something about this.* This thought pattern may be more easily understood by analyzing a situation that happened to me.

This morning I was in freak-out mode. I didn't have much time. It was T-minus ten minutes until we needed to be out the door—and my son needed water, my daughter wanted me to braid her hair, and I wasn't even dressed yet. I tried to balance it all with ease, but I was starting to sweat. Plus, I'd just read an email from a customer service rep. There was some sort of "issue" with my account. Apparently they needed me to log in to their service, review my past purchases, and set up some sort of account fraud monitoring. My website had been hacked; I'd tried to log in, but the website wasn't working. It was loading and loading. All this was hitting me before breakfast. Of course, after that failed login attempt, I was all nerves. My son was trying to talk to me; I couldn't hear. My mind was somewhere else. I was still scrolling my emails, trying to get more information—but then I got sidetracked by another email. Someone needed more information for another project I was working on. My chest tightened. *I have to get myself together. There is so much to do.* It also was my husband's birthday. *I should be making this day amazing for him. How can I even do all this? I need to be in the car already.*

Ahh! My insides wanted to scream. *I should be doing better. I should be doing more. The kids should be at school early. It is testing week. I'm supposed to give them a huge breakfast. I only have three more days to complete this book and—is it even good? What am I doing for my husband's birthday? How do I do it all?*

After hastily getting dressed, trying to throw on some worship music to calm my nerves, and effectively feeding my kids' hungry faces with bagels and cream cheese, I plopped into the car, ready to go. No keys. I nervously ran back inside, heart pumping. I frantically grabbed a cup of coffee off my counter and located the keys. I sprinted back to the car. The coffee tasted bad. I threw it out. *I have to do everything*, I thought.

Meanwhile my husband and kids were waiting patiently inside the car—and my nerves were reverberating through my chest as I got back in the car.

"Peace," my husband said.

"Roar!" I wanted to say back.

"We are all good," I announced to my family, trying to fix my own lack of good emotions. But my words really should've been translated to, "I'm saying I'm good right now, but I'm really not good at all!"

My kids deserved a comforting hug before their big testing day. My husband deserved better on his birthday. My anxiety was through the roof. I was faking being okay, which was lying. My attitude was deplorable. I hated it when I did this to myself.

Underneath it all, I wondered, *How do I fix me? How do I stop feeling this way? How do I fix everything?*

Let's work through our two-part process as it pertains to my thought.

STOP

1. Capture the Thought

My thought was: *I have to do everything myself.* In the same vein are the following thoughts: *I have to do ___. I have to perform or work to be loved. I have to act holy to be seen as holy. I have to look good. I have to handle everything. I have to make people get in line. I have to go after the things I want. I have to*

194

be a Martha and move! I have to appear better or do better than what I am doing right now.

Do you ever experience thoughts like these? Do you ever feel burdened, rushed, overwhelmed, over-responsible, or pressured?

I felt: stress, anxiety, panic, and rush.

2. Determine Who Is Speaking

Who is speaking? God? My flesh? Or the enemy?

A good place to start when thinking this through is, What fruit is coming forth from the thought? Does the thought lead to peace? Joy? Patience? Any other fruit of the Spirit?

If it doesn't, the thought is likely not from the mind of Christ. In my case, there was no fruit from feeling overwhelmed, only an overabundance of stress.

Was it my flesh speaking this thought? Certainly, the flesh wants to be comfortable. The flesh wants everything handled. The flesh wants all things wrapped up with a pretty little bow and smiles on everyone's faces. The flesh hates process and growth time. It wants to be at the destination already. Yes, in large part, my reactions were motivated by the flesh.

Was the enemy, the accuser of my soul, speaking? While I didn't blatantly hear accusations, I remember how the enemy speaks in Scripture:

> [The devil] said to [himself],
> > "I will ascend to heaven and set my throne above God's
> > > stars.
> > I will preside on the mountain of the gods
> > > far away in the north.
> > I will climb to the highest heavens
> > > and be like the Most High." (Isa. 14:13–14 NLT)

The devil says, *Kelly, go ahead. Do it yourself, apart from God. Make your way. Rather than trusting God, step ahead of Him and do it yourself. Raise up your own throne. You know what to do. Don't be a passive nincompoop. Do something! It'll be a whole lot faster if you do it anyway.*

Recognizing who is speaking gives me cause for pause. When I step in front of God to handle things, I block God's assistance. Upon reflection, I realize I am called to move out of the way so He can deal with my family members and friends. Pride blocks His move. And it prohibits His best results—both for myself and in the lives of those around me.

I don't want to block God.

When I overexert myself, I get an underrated result. This is the grimy water the devil wants to lead me to. *Handle it*, he says. But I don't have to listen to him.

My nine-year-old daughter is famous for saying, "Shut up, devil!" I can say that too. And move myself out of God's way.

I am not raising up my own throne; I am raising up Jesus's via a mind submitted to the mind of Christ. In this, I can move myself into a posture of understanding His leading so I can produce an abundance of fruit, not a pile of fret.

Who might be speaking to you in moments like these? How can you produce fruit by yielding to the mind of Christ instead of fretting?

3. Understand Intent

If the thought, *I have to step in and do something about this* is left unchecked, where will it lead me in five, ten, or thirty years?

Doing what is not of God leads away from God.

It is arrogant for me to think I can force God's hand. It is prideful to think I can will and work better than the King of Kings. It is presuming to figure I have the best solutions. It is impatient to jump in and act before He does.

For jealousy and selfishness are not God's kind of wisdom. Such things are earthly, unspiritual, and **demonic**. For wherever there is jealousy and selfish ambition, there you will find disorder and evil of every kind. (James 3:15–16 NLT)

When selfishness, jealousy, and selfish ambition rule, we begin to kill those God may want us to reach. Impatience turns to slander. Aggravation becomes gossip. Assumptions make us accusers. We curse, we complain, and we demand better—all while pressing harder into our thoughts and plan, not God's. The adversary of our soul loves this behavior!

Thirty years down the road, where will this sort of behavior leave us? Doused in stress and tension, perhaps filled with sickness of body, troubled and anxious in our minds, and grieved in spirit. Certainly this road leads to anger and bitterness. The body wasn't designed to carry this load of stress.

The flesh-driven mind, without the Spirit, leads to death (Rom. 8:6). These thoughts and moves don't only end up killing and slandering others but boomerang back, killing and slandering us because we sidestepped God and because we didn't do things right.

The devil is out to kill us when we move away from trusting Jesus. He aims to get us to try to save ourselves, but we already have a Savior. Wisdom always returns to Jesus and averts trouble.

START

1. Submit to the Mind of Christ

I adore the King by praying:

Father God, I thank You that You are the God of all the universe. You are in ultimate control of all things. You have the whole world—all its princes, all its kings, all governments—in the palm of Your hand. All things are under Your authority and jurisdiction. Jesus is reigning and ruling as King. His rule is good and right. I submit myself to His rule and His authority. I come into agreement with all the ways of the Father, Son, and Holy Spirit and, by the grace of Jesus, allow them to have their way in my life. I trust You. I choose to lean not on my own mind, so I can gain Your mind about this thought. Come, Holy Spirit, and teach me. Come, Holy Spirit, and lead me. Your way is better. Have Your way. I submit and surrender afresh. I want to change and grow more and more into Your image, so the very thoughts of Christ are my thoughts. In Jesus's name. Amen.

As I spend time with God and think about having to do everything myself or needing to do something, a Scripture pops in my head:

> Some trust in chariots and some in horses,
> but we trust in the name of the LORD our God.
> (Ps. 20:7)

Here, I realize even my best plan is foolishness compared to the plan of Him who carries the name of the Lord. Who will I rely on? Will I pray, or will I just assume I should do things my way?

> Unless the LORD builds the house,
> the builders labor in vain.
> Unless the LORD watches over the city,
> the guards stand watch in vain. (127:1)

If God doesn't build what I put my hands to, what a waste! All I'll create is something that is of no value. This is called vanity, and vanity does not produce fruit.

What else does the Holy Spirit want me to know? A familiar truth comes to mind: Jesus is the Author, Source, and Finisher (see Heb. 12:2 AMPC). This verse reminds me that when I jump in and force my own endings, I cut off the story line Jesus is developing and finishing. (Remember John the Baptist and Jesus's baptism?

Remember Peter and the foot washing?) To jump ahead of God is arrogance. Even if I have to sit around learning and leaning on Jesus—and feel like I am not adding any value or that I have no significance—if that is what Jesus wants, if this is His will for me at this time, then it is good. God will reward my obedience. He will reward yours too.

To follow Jesus is to go down a path that will not look like you expected. Remember when Jesus went to Samaria and it made no sense to the disciples? Getting out of our minds is getting into the mind of Christ.

Again, Romans 12:2 tells us, "Don't copy the behavior and customs of this world, but let God transform you into a new person by changing [transforming] the way you think. Then you will learn to know God's will for you, which is good and pleasing and perfect" (NLT).

Cheerlead your soul. Stir up your faith. Declare these things over your life, and other truths as you are prompted by the Holy Spirit:

Father, "your kingdom come, your will be done" (Matt. 6:10) in my life.

I will "be still in the presence of the LORD, and wait patiently for [You] to act" (Ps. 37:7 NLT).

I believe "better is one day in your courts than a thousand elsewhere" (84:10).

I know all things are working together for good, for I love God and "have been called according to his purpose" (Rom. 8:28).

I "seek first his kingdom and his righteousness, and all these things will be given to [me] as well" (Matt. 6:33).

As I follow You, the Prince of Peace, I can trust You to lead me in the way to go as I follow paths of peace.

2. Discover Any Unlocked Doors

What unlocked this behavior and thought in me? What made me prone to fix, to handle, to rush in? What past circumstances or beliefs created this situation?

I admit I don't like feeling out of control. I don't like the roller-coaster ride of an uncertain future. It's uncomfortable and scary. I like knowing. I like achieving. I like having a handle on life.

Are you anything like me?

Busyness, bossiness, and bold advice are my inner comforts. They fill the gaps I am uncomfortable with. They protect me from feeling out of control. They seem to give me value as a person. They make me feel like I have a handle on life. They make me look in charge.

But I have to ask myself, *Do these coping strategies work?*

Do they help me or keep me from reliance on God? Do they protect me or injure me? Do they give me peace or grip my heart with the burden of getting a good result?

Rather than attempting to hold up the world with our own bare hands, I think a better solution is to admit our pressing fear to the Lord. It is to admit that we don't know. It is to say, "God, You are going to have to handle this, because I feel completely and utterly out of control."

Concealing pain hurts us, but revealing it to Jesus heals us.

To unlock the door today, I admit that I am afraid of feeling uncomfortable, awkward, or in need. I ask God to forgive me.

What might you need to admit to the Savior? What might God heal in you as you confess fear or pride?

3. Repent, Renounce, and Pray

Father God, wow. I am sorry. Sometimes I want what You do for me more than I want You. I want results. I want answers. I want the benefits of You without relationship. I am guilty. Running away and hiding is not helping me; doing this is hurting me. I repent of being led by my own mind and working up my own proactive actions. I also bind the enemy, who wants me to bite apples that are just fix-it schemes. He knows how to appeal to my flesh, but my flesh doesn't have to obey when I am obedient to the life-giving Spirit. Fill me afresh with Your Spirit. Give me a mind to be led by the Spirit. Even more, I repent of all actions of manipulation, control, self-centeredness, fear, and self-will. I rebuke the enemy. I renounce strongholds of self-will aiming to lead me to rebellion, jealousy, selfish ambition, hatred, and discord. I pray, Father, for You to take those down right now. I submit to Your way, Your will, and Your timing, no matter how uncomfortable it makes me feel. I also bind the enemy and his attacks. I no longer want self-reliance; I want God-dependence. I break the agreement that I have the best way. I break the agreement that You take too long. I break the agreement that I have to make my own breakthrough happen. I ask that, now, You would make me more ready to submit to Your Holy Spirit. I proclaim my trust in Your leadership. You are the Commander, the Orchestrator, and the Author of my life. I want my life to be in right order before You, Lord of Lords. I will not yoke up again to the flesh. Flesh is always hungry. I don't have to feed it. I have the Word of God, which is the Bread of Life. I am sustained. You are more than enough. Your verdicts are right. Your ways are right. Your timeline is right. I come into full agreement with Your plan and Your heart for me. In Jesus's name, I pray. Amen.

4. Go a New Way

"In the multitude of my [anxious] thoughts within me, Your comforts cheer and delight my soul!" (Ps. 94:19 AMPC). There is comfort available for our chaotic times and thoughts. The Holy Spirit is our Comforter (John 14:16 KJV). The mind of Christ delivers us solutions of peace. Why is this important? Because who can hear when "flight or fight, eat or be eaten" kicks in? No one can. Scientifically, at that moment the mind is just trying to stay alive. It is hard to talk to someone who is losing it.

But we as believers have the mind of Christ. To abide with Jesus, we carry peace. And peace settles things.

> And let the peace (soul harmony which comes) from Christ rule (act as umpire continually) in your hearts [deciding and settling with finality all questions that arise in your minds, in that peaceful state] to which as [members of Christ's] one body you were also called [to live]. And be thankful (appreciative), [giving praise to God always]. (Col. 3:15 AMPC)

When we carry peace, we start praising instead of worrying. We go about discerning instead of fighting. We get praying instead of fixing everything. We begin speaking like Jesus instead of handling the world based on our whims. We stay connected with God. We continue in trust—and we know this trust will not disappoint us.

> And you shall know [with an acquaintance and understanding based on and grounded in personal experience] that I am the Lord; for they shall not be put to shame who wait for, look for, hope for, and expect Me. (Isa. 49:23 AMPC)

We wait, despite our flesh demanding we move. We hope, knowing that at the right time God will give us *His answer*. We expect, and we look for doors of escape put in place by God (1 Cor. 10:13). We *ginosko* know that God will show up, because we've experienced His just-in-time moves before. God doesn't put His kids to shame.

We wait on the Lord.

5. Keep the Temple Shining

As we move out from here, we must be wise. The enemy loves to condemn flesh that waits on the Lord. Don't listen to him.

For instance, I may be led by God to ask for more help from my family instead of fuming internally. They may willingly help me load up the dishes, put their clothes in the hamper, and be amazing! Yet the enemy can still speak. He may still say something like, *You aren't doing enough as a mom.*

Wise people are aware of the retaliation of the enemy. They have a rebuttal ready. In my case, I'd say back, *I don't have to do everything. Christ already did. His grace is enough!*

At this point, I tell myself, *I reject all condemnation. If Jesus said there is "no condemnation" in Him (Rom. 8:1), then there is none.* Likely, I pray here and say: "God, I trust You. I trust You to keep me and to lead me. I am not perfect, but You are helping me. You love me right here where I am. You see my heart and how I am doing the best I can do. I thank You, God, for Your help. Your grace is enough! I am free. You will lead me in all things."

Beyond this, I may also apply the Word of God practically to my life. In this case, I may think: *If God took time to rest while creating the whole earth in seven days, I can rest too. Rest is part of the creation process. Rest actually creates new things.*

I am not selfish to reassure myself that I am wise, because this is how I will persist in faith, hope, and love. Using the Word of God, the sword of the Spirit, to build me up, I move forward. I take up my shield of faith by expecting God will help me in tough moments.

David, a man after God's own heart, knew this sort of comforting, experiential love, because he knew God's heart. David said it best, as he declared this faith-building statement to his soul and spirit:

> I'm sure now I'll see God's goodness
> in the exuberant earth.

Stay with GOD!
  Take heart. Don't quit.
I'll say it again:
  Stay with GOD. (Ps. 27:13–14 MSG)

I won't quit. I won't back down. God will help me. This I know!

16

An Overcomer's Guide to Keeping Thoughts Captive

One thing I can't stand is vagueness. There is always the chance, when we talk about spiritual things, that it becomes subjective versus actively implementable. I hate that. I hate the idea of you closing this book without being armed with an active way to stand firm and go forth. My job is to give you every tool you need to succeed, by God's power.

The previous chapters addressed five lies that commonly plague believers. I used my story as a template, but I hope you've grasped how to make the Stop/Start Process directly implementable as it pertains to your own thoughts.

Why not take some time and address some of the lies you are believing right now? There is no time better than now; tomorrow is always a day ahead of immediate impact. Grab a journal and press in. If you need a little more help walking this out, remember that I have created a worksheet for you that spells out the process. You can find the "Take Every Thought Captive Worksheet" at www.itakethoughtscaptive.com.

Also, to make this near-final chapter 100 percent implementable, I've organized it as a practical guide for you full of tips, common thoughts, and wisdom to use when brutal attacks, issues, or questions pop into your head. More than anything, I want you to feel like you have firm footing to stand on going forward.

Some of you may be inclined to skip the last chapter. In many books, the last chapter is only a summary wrapping things up with a pretty bow. That is not the case in this book. You will need these tips. Don't read them later; read them now. Don't plan on coming back to them when you hit a hard time. That's too late. Read them now—*and* later. Know how to handle problem situations before trouble hits.

To prepare for war is to get your armor on. Do that now, so you don't get hit later.

After you've already gotten yourself into a hot mental mess, it's likely too late. What you don't know won't help you. Know *now* so you can think right later. Know *now* so you can spend weeks creating new neural pathways with this sort of thinking. Then, when the big attack comes, you'll have already gone to boot camp and will easily be able to win. Spend the time rereading the chapters you need help with. Through the mind of Christ teaching and guiding you, walk out a new way of thinking and living.

These ten points offer wisdom to help us defeat the worst mental quagmires. They address hindrances that get our minds knotted up and help us know the way to go. They offer practical how-to help. They take down stronghold issues we may not even realize we have. And the bonus one we'll end with gives us an important key we will need going forward.

Plan to prevail; do not prepare, by doing nothing, to fail.

Let's go!

1. What to Think in the Gap of Not Knowing What to Think

By this point in the book, you know what *not* to think. But in the gap of not thinking, there can be a void. Voids become vacuums. Vacuums suck up junk. We don't want junk; we want God and godliness in our minds.

When we don't know what to think, what do we think?

Finally, brothers and sisters, whatever is true, whatever is noble, whatever is right, whatever is pure, whatever is lovely, whatever is admirable—if anything is excellent or praiseworthy—think about such things. (Phil. 4:8)

In the gap of thoughts removed, think about:

What you love.

What good has happened.

The good God has for you.

What is worthy of praise.

What is excellent.

To think on what is good is to remember God's goodness and faithfulness. It is to stay united with the mind of Christ.

When you start to think bad thoughts, return to goodness. Don't speak what is untrue, wrong, impure, unlovely, horrible, and so on. If you speak it, you've already thought it. If you watch it on TV, you will think about it. Guard yourself. Above all else, guard that heart of yours, so your mind will be a full-out temple of the living Lord.

The eye is the lamp of the body. If your eyes are healthy, your whole body will be full of light. But if your eyes are unhealthy, your whole body will be full of darkness. If then the light within you is darkness, how great is that darkness! (Matt. 6:22–23)

Does this seem like too high of a calling? Following Jesus *is* a high calling. Embrace that now, rather than conforming to and compromising with the world. And remember: it is not your strength but His that will empower you.

Journal: God, what are You speaking to me? What are You calling me to? How do I do this?

---

2. What to Do When a Mental Attack Hits

Friend, you need to know and remember that you are not living a lighthearted weekend trip. You aren't on a walk through the park.

> This is no weekend war that we'll walk away from and forget about in a couple of hours. This is for keeps, a life-or-death fight to the finish against the Devil and all his angels. (Eph. 6:11–12 MSG)

What rages around us is real war. Don't be fooled into thinking this is just another day. There is a real destroyer after your life named Satan. He doesn't mess around or go at it easy. He isn't looking to be your friend and work with you. He wants to rip your life apart from the inside out.

When you feel an attack coming on, STOP and take a stand.

> Be prepared. You're up against far more than you can handle on your own. Take all the help you can get, every weapon God has

208

issued, so that when it's all over but the shouting you'll still be on your feet. (vv. 13–14 MSG)

When you feel oppression, when you feel torment, when you feel anguish, do not hesitate! Resist the enemy. Fight the good fight in your mind. Quickly take your thoughts captive.

Be prepared. Use the weapons God has given you and put on the armor Christ has afforded you. Don't be negligent.

Wear at all times the armor of Ephesians 6:13–17:

- Truth is a belt that holds you above the fray of demonic fights.
- Peace is a gentle-flowing river, no matter what words, fights, schemes, or torrents you walk into.
- Salvation keeps your mind and thoughts secure as you trust the Lord to save.
- Righteousness is a guard over your heart. Know you truly are holy, righteous, and blameless in God's sight (thanks to Jesus).
- Faith in God's protection is a shield that will block targeted attacks coming at you.
- The Word of God is your sword, a weapon you can wield and use.

Be specific about your cover. Start your day with firm resolve. Pray about following peace, if that's your issue. Memorize Scripture that talks about your righteousness if that's the place the enemy hits every time. If you need an extra dose of faith, read stories of people in the Bible whose faith carried them through. Don't just do nothing; do something. If you want something changed, you must meet God with a hunger, trusting Him to change it. This is how minds get renewed. When we do what the Holy Spirit has for us to do and STAND ON IT, then our minds and hearts are impenetrable.

Journal: God, what are You speaking to me? What are You calling me to? How do I do this?

---

3. What to Do When Emotions Try to Take Over

Most of the time, we think bad then feel bad. But did you know the opposite also happens? Bad feelings can create bad thoughts.

How many of us have woken up on the wrong side of the bed? We feel *blah*, and so we start to complain in our minds. The day is about to be horrible. We don't want to do what is ahead. We hate our lives. Our bad feeling created bad thoughts.

I've realized we must not only take thoughts captive but feelings, too, lest they turn into thoughts. How?

Here is what I do when a debilitating feeling hits: I smile BIG. I smile huge, and I choose to feel joy deep down. When I do this, something shifts in me. I actually feel happy. This is not fake joy; I am loved. And because I am loved, I can be full of joy.

Jesus said, "These things I have spoken to you, that my joy may be in you, and that your joy may be full" (John 15:11 ESV). Here I can say, "The joy of the Lord is [my] strength" (Neh. 8:10), just like Nehemiah did.

This choice to feel joy cuts off depressive or depleting enemy attacks.

Is this denying my feelings? No. I can confront the issue later. But not every issue is worth confronting. Rely on the mind of Christ for how to go forward. He will not lead you wrong.

Don't let a molehill-sized thought become a mountain-sized monster. Just because our world is constantly offended, it doesn't mean we have to be. Just because news and world issues feel so pressing, it doesn't mean we have to be pressed. We have power! We can make decisions on what we let in and what we keep out. Choose rightly. Do not forsake God's calling because some urgent issue demands you worry about it. Do not allow your mind to be consumed and used that way.

Instead, smile, look at that feeling, and say, "You're a feeling, not my Ruler and Maker." Forbid a feeling from forming your day or your outlook. God made your day, and He has good in it for you. Period.

Furthermore, when an attack hits, be willing to receive help. I am struck by how Jesus received help when Simon carried His cross for Him. Jesus could have said, "No thanks, I am the King of Kings and Lord of Lords." But He didn't. He had all power, but still He accepted help.

If Jesus, the Son of God, full of all power and authority, received help, what message does that send us? We don't always have to be strong. Be willing to accept help.

The body of Christ needs the body of Christ. Some of us are saying, "Why am I struggling so much? Why isn't God helping me?"

Well, He is. You just aren't picking up the phone when His messenger, your friend from your small group, is calling to pray for you.

Receive from the body—and give to it, too, so the body of Christ is a strong body, not a wounded one.

Your emotions don't have to be the boss of you. The joy of Jesus and a good friend are fantastic pick-me-ups when the going gets tough.

Journal: God, what are You speaking to me? What are You calling me to? How do I do this?

_____

_____

_____

_____

_____

_____

4. How to Make Mentally Tough Decisions

Have you ever gotten a mental headache because you don't know what to do? How do you make a hard decision? One of the hardest things to feel is *torn*.

When I find myself in this place, this one verse has helped me so much: "Do everything in love" (1 Cor. 16:14).

I am called to love God. And to love other people as myself.

Jesus said, "'Love the Lord your God with all your heart and with all your soul and with all your mind and with all your strength. . . . Love your neighbor as yourself.' There is no commandment greater than these" (Mark 12:30–31).

When confronting a decision, there is wisdom in asking the question, God, will this further love?

Will this action further my love of God, or will it block it? Will it allow me to love others more? Will it be loving toward myself? Will it allow me to love like Jesus loved? Will it be following peace, since Jesus is the Prince of Peace and we are followers of Jesus?

We do not want to get love confused with religious obligation. If we act because we are burdened and obligated, if we sigh under our breath as we do something, we must ask ourselves, Does this

212

act really have a heart of love behind it? Usually this sort of thing is rooted in fear or in people pleasing.

Evaluate your heart, and ask yourself:

Am I moving out of real love or obligation?

Am I doing this from selfish ambition or God-centered inspiration?

Is the Prince of Peace in this decision?

Is this about God or myself?

Have I listened to the mind of Christ while setting down my own objectives?

Am I doing this to please people, or because God is calling me to it?

Also, it is helpful to ask, What option is most likely to produce the fruit of the Spirit: love, joy, peace, patience, kindness, goodness, faithfulness, gentleness, and self-control?

"Love never fails" (1 Cor. 13:8). Decisions rooted in love can't fail. Isn't that reassuring? Move from the place of love.

Journal: God, what are You speaking to me? What are You calling me to? How do I do this?

5. How to Process Passive-Aggressive Actions

The social event was supposed to include me, but it didn't. Post-event, without much explanation as to why things happened the way they did, I texted the individual involved to get more understanding.

I asked, "What happened?"

Their response? An emoji. What kind of explanation is that? What does an emoji face even mean? Was there a subliminal message behind this face? I supposed the person wanted to say to me, *Get over yourself already.*

I felt stupid for caring so much. Apparently, they didn't care as much as I did. I decided, *They don't care for me. They don't like me. They only care about their goals.* I personalized. And, without the full story being known, personalization quickly partners with lies.

I texted the person again, wanting to know what happened. Only truth sets us free.

No response.

Hmm . . . what do I do?

I remembered how I had personalized in the past. The majority of the times that I made assumptions, I got things wrong.

Maybe this person who lacked a good response was busy or going through a struggle. Maybe they felt horrible. I really don't know anything until I hear something straight from their mouth.

I decided to fall back on Scripture: "*Make allowance for each other's faults,* and forgive anyone who offends you" (Col. 3:13 NLT).

Demanding this person answer me is not my business. My business is to forgive and to move on so that I can continue to abide with Christ. My goal is always to stay connected to the mind of Christ.

In this, I chose to mentally hear what I believe they would have wanted to say. It sounded something like this: "Kelly, we love you so much. With so much going on around us, we got distracted and things didn't pan out the way we hoped. We feel really bad about that."

How can you think the best of others? How can you see their heart through the eyes of Christ? What would that look like?

There is always a heart behind the no or the odd response, even if we can't hear it. Hear God's heart and His grace. Think as Jesus thinks. His blood always speaks a better word. From the cross, Jesus said, "Father, forgive them, for they do not know what they are doing" (Luke 23:34). Jesus is in us, and His Word is still speaking.

I chose to move forward in love, even if words of apology would never come. Why? Because love frees me—more than holding a grudge ever will. Love covers a multitude of sins. Love cannot fail.

We are the most full of love when we are extending love and forgiveness to others. How might we be called to overlook an offense? How can we avoid presuming we know the message tucked in between the lines of what seem like passive-aggressive sentences?

What if instead of cursing people in our minds we were to believe the best? Often, the way we *don't* want to be treated can serve as a great lesson. We can offer the grace we wish others would extend us.

How can we handle passive-aggressive behavior before it starts? These three things help:

- Clarify expectations from both parties up front.
- Check in with the person often to be sure that everyone is on the same page.
- Take responsibility for anything not going right. Apologize if necessary, and communicate next steps clearly.

We cannot change others, but we can do our part to be honest and forthright. Doing this will help us divert mental accidents before they happen.

Journal: God, what are You speaking to me? What are You calling me to? How do I do this?

---

6. How to Handle Stray Thoughts

This morning, as I was sitting talking with my husband, a day-dream-thought popped in my head. In it, another man was talking to me at a location where I might be going to. It seemed like he wanted to have a relationship with me.

Where did this image come from, and why was I thinking it? I don't go around thinking about other men, not at all. I could feel shame, but I knew better—this wasn't my thought!

This was an enemy thought. I have no interest in other men. I do not look at other guys. I am not desiring another relationship. I do not want out of my marriage.

In situations like these, we can do two things:

1. *We can say, "Get away from me, Satan. I am not interested in this."* When the enemy showed up, Jesus said, "Get behind me, Satan!" (Matt. 16:23). We can do the same, and can instantly shut down attacks by recognizing them for what they are and moving them out. Here, we don't take things personally. We move on.

2. *We can bounce!* I tell my kids that, when they are at school, if someone says something mean to them, they

can say, "Bounce!" The words don't have to stick—like a basketball on pavement. When we say, "Bounce," whatever the thought was doesn't have to stick to us. We immediately bounce off that thought and move on.

In my situation, I "bounced." I didn't make it a big deal. I didn't dwell on it. I said, "Whatever!" and moved on.

Journal: God, what are You speaking to me? What are You calling me to? How do I do this?

7. How to Stop Judgmental Thoughts

I screamed as loudly as I could at my third-grade daughter's basketball game. Her team was down by too many points. *They* needed *to make a basket—now!*

Sitting on the edge of my seat, I noticed a girl on her team was being a ball hog. Another kept dribbling the basketball forever, just standing there. *Doesn't she know how to pass?* "Pass! Pass!" I screamed. *What's wrong with this girl?*

Right after I screamed—there it was. Something hit me. Was it a still, small voice? These words landed in my mind: *It's easy to be a critic from the sidelines.*

217

Wow. That was true. I wasn't on the court. I didn't see from the same angle those girls did. It was easy for me to criticize without spending a minute in the game.

I was not the one with the ball. I couldn't see what it looked like from their vantage point. I had no understanding of what it felt like to have gone up and down the court thirty times already.

How often do I judge, from the sidelines, what people in the game should do?

My husband's work. A church person's actions. An online comment.

I judge in a minute when I haven't walked a moment in their shoes. Yet I have no idea the mud and muck someone's walked through to get where they are. It is always easy to be a critic.

So, what do I do here?

I don't have some four-step plan for beating criticism; I still struggle with it at times. But I think a big first step is to "shutteth ye trappeth" (be it in mind or mouth).

> The mouths of fools are their undoing,
>   and their lips are a snare to their very lives. (Prov. 18:7)

Our mouths are a trap. It is better to keep them shut. It is better to refrain from getting on a court we haven't been invited on and instead stay focused on our game—a game of love. To stay on the court God is calling us to play on.

In the instance of my daughter's game, I was called to be her biggest fan. I dropped that ball when I started looking at other girls. I moved out of the mind of Christ and into criticism instead.

Jesus always loved, redeemed, blessed, healed, and helped. He always focused on what the Father was doing. He knew His mission. He kept His eye on the prize. He did not get deterred.

I can do the same. I can keep my eye on my mission, hear from the mind of Christ, and trust others are in the Lord's hands. He is God enough to take care of them.

Journal: God, what are You speaking to me? What are You calling me to? How do I do this?

---

8. How to Avoid Thought-Triggering Bait

Did you know we are constantly presented with lures? The enemy is always dropping a line down into the water of our world. He wants to see if we will bite.

He knows our favorite variety of lure too. He knows what snags us. For some it is shopping. For others it is alcohol. For many it is busyness.

What is your lure? And what does any of this have to do with your mind?

Everything.

If the destroyer of our souls can snag us in thought, he will effectively snag us in action. How many of us have determined to stop doing something? We will stop smoking. We will stop eating chips for breakfast. We will stop talking rudely and judgmentally. (Ahem, that's me.)

But then the lure falls, right in our faces. We see it. We taste it. We bite it! We devour it—hook, line, and sinker. *Ahh!* The fruit is ripe, our feelings demand a reaction, and we can't help ourselves—or so it seems.

Before long, the mental consequences of our actions set in. *I'm bad. God doesn't like me anymore.* Such thoughts put distance between us and God. Distance welcomes in disillusionment, doubt, and confusion.

What do we do? Repent.

Repentance is our only door of escape if we've landed in disillusionment, doubt, or confusion—but hopefully we won't land in those places at all.

Better than having to look back at sin is not getting into sin to begin with. This saves us from a whole lot of tears, stress, agonizing, and regrets.

Don't take the bait.

How? Be aware of what bait the enemy uses against you. What does it mentally look like when you get lured in? What happens? What triggers continually bait you?

If you skip workouts because you don't have enough time, get ahead of the issue by setting your alarm clock. If you miss workouts because you forget, put your shoes in the hallway to your bathroom the night before.

Proactively plan so you don't reactively bite the lure. For instance, the lure may be thoughts such as, *I feel antsy. I can't relax. I feel stressed.*

The bait: the bottle of wine on the counter. Soon, you grab it. One drink becomes three. Your promise to God to stop drinking is ruined. You hate yourself.

Don't do this any longer. Throw out the wine the night before. Remember, we don't keep snakes as pets. We nail them to the wall and have done with them.

What is your plan? Win the war before it starts!

Journal: God, what are You speaking to me? What are You calling me to? How do I do this?

9. How to Handle Deep Disappointment or Despair

My mind flashed back to a conversation I had with my son over breakfast months ago. I said to him, "Son, because God is so amazing, every disappointment has very great potential to be a God-appointment."[1]

I reminded my son of people in the Bible such as Joseph, who was literally in a pit only to see God bring him to a palace years later, with true character of heart. I told him how Moses experienced plagues only to gain freedom for his people via those exact deliverance-focused plagues. I reminded my son how probably no one understood Noah and his big ole boat, yet it delivered the animals and his family to safe and dry land.

Disappointment makes us feel blocked, but trust in God delivers hope that good can come out of bad. A spring can emerge out of a rock. A parting of the waves can part a sea. A Savior can be born and placed in a manger.

The exact words the Lord supplied me to deliver to my son are also delivering me. God has good for me.

What about you? Has your life been a big bag of disappointment?

My friend, these words I am about to write are not a cliché: God is greater than any disappointment you have ever faced. This fact does not negate your journey, your hard road. I know it's been tough. I know there have been tears. I've been there too.

But the reality remains: God is greater. He is greater than what you haven't seen yet. He is greater than what you think will happen. He is greater than any season you walk through. He is greater than what you are upset at yourself about. Do not allow your disappointment to define you. Remember Christ in you—the hope of ALL glory is inside you!

Plus, God is our Redeemer. Everything He does is about redemption and restoration. Countless people in the Bible—if not almost all of them—had to wait for redemption to come.

Think about the cross. Three dark, uncertain days. How disappointed did the disciples feel? How discouraged?

Don't give up hope in your wait.

> They who wait for the LORD shall renew their strength;
>   they shall mount up with wings like eagles;
> they shall run and not be weary;
>   they shall walk and not faint. (Isa. 40:31 ESV)

Journal: God, what are You speaking to me? What are You calling me to? How do I do this?

10. How to Stop Thinking, *I'm Too Late*

Once upon a time, there was a girl who figured she was too late to catch the bus. The clock read 8:05, and she was still all snuggled up in her warm bed, under the safety of cool covers. Sure, she could hustle and throw clothes on, but surely she'd miss the bus, which came at 8:10. She was behind now; why bother?

She just lay there, not moving. Stationary. Defeated.

I'm late again. I missed it—again.

Little did she know that the bus was also running behind. She wouldn't have had five minutes to get ready, but ten—and that would have made all the difference.

Instead, she thought, *I hate myself.*

Many of us figure we've missed the bus when we haven't. There are a million reasons why we haven't missed it, but all we can see are the thousand reasons why we are too late, washed up, out of touch, or out of God's plan.

God is an on-time God. He can instantly take you where you are meant to go. Don't put up with the mental torment that says you've missed your bus.

One day, when Jesus hopped in the boat with the disciples, they instantly got where they needed to go. If Jesus did that with them, can't He do that with you? Reflect on these verses:

> That evening Jesus' disciples went down to the shore to wait for him. But as darkness fell and Jesus still hadn't come back, they got into the boat and headed across the lake toward Capernaum. Soon a gale swept down upon them, and the sea grew very rough. They had rowed three or four miles when suddenly they saw Jesus walking on the water toward the boat. They were terrified, but he called out to them, "Don't be afraid. I am here!" Then they were **eager to let him in the boat, and immediately they arrived at their destination!** (John 6:16–21 NLT)

When Jesus gets in the boat, you get where you need to go. Storms are no issue. Darkness is no issue. Timing is no issue. When the King of Kings comes in, you get where He is taking you.

Journal: God, what are You speaking to me? What are You calling me to? How do I do this?

_____

_____

_____

_____

The ONE THING You Must Carry with You at All Times

In this book you have learned a whole lot about what not to think and how to think in union with the mind of Christ. But where do you go from here? How do you carry on along your journey with faith high and fear low?

You pray at all times, without ceasing. "Pray in the Spirit at all times and on every occasion. Stay alert and be persistent in your prayers for all believers everywhere" (Eph. 6:18 NLT).

Pray. And then pray some more. And pray also for the persecuted church, other believers, Jesus's body and bride as a whole, what is on God's heart, and God's kingdom come to earth.

And when you pray, believe! With lack of faith, your prayers can be at great risk of becoming wasted words.

> Only it must be in faith that he asks with no wavering (no hesitating, no doubting). For the one who wavers (hesitates, doubts) is like the billowing surge out at sea that is blown hither and thither and tossed by the wind.
>
> For truly, let not such a person imagine that he will receive anything [he asks for] from the Lord, [for being as he is] a man of two minds (hesitating, dubious, irresolute), [he is] unstable and unreliable and uncertain about everything [he thinks, feels, decides]. (James 1:6–8 AMPC)

Prayer lassos a mind and harnesses it to the intents and purposes of God.

It takes down the enemy. It opens doors no one else can close. It brings the supernatural to pass, despite how horrible the natural circumstances seem. Prayer—connected prayer to God—is your way!

If you don't pray, rest assured the enemy will prey on you. That's just a fact. Prayer puts air cover over you. Enlist the heavenlies in your battle to take every thought captive.

Prayer is clarity that pushes away confusion. Regularly submit your whole being to Jesus as your Lord. When you pray, you remind all of yourself who is in charge.

I pray things like, "In the name of Jesus, I submit my mind, my thoughts, my heart, and everything I am to my Lord Jesus Christ. I give Jesus full reign in my life in all His ways. I lay down my way for Your way, Jesus, and I choose to trust You today in everything."

Also, you have to be wise and discerning about the war going on around you. Sometimes war enters our minds through other people; they come to us with troubles or fears that feel sticky. Like they just got glued on us. Be aware of that, and pray it away.

In these times, I pray something like, "Father, I thank You that I was able to love and listen to ____. I bless them, and I ask that any of their worry, fear, or remnants of their sin be washed off me right now by Your living water. I let go of what issues belong to them to carry now. I also ask that You, Father God, would help them with all those things. I receive only what is Your heart and mind for me at this time."

Usually when I pray this, I feel the residue go. And then, in the future, I use wisdom as I am led by the Holy Spirit when conversations start to feel icky. I do not fear others. In fact, I have had to cut a person's dialogue short when my Holy Spirit–led conscience threw off a red alert: *Too much! Too many lurid details! Be warned, be wise.*

Or, when a friend started to gossip, I simply said to them, "I am sorry. I am feeling convicted about this conversation, and so to protect my heart I am going to stop talking about this right now. Let's talk about something else."

Essentially, I say to people, between the lines, "I honor your story, but I don't think I have to hear this part and all the details to know what you are trying to say." I don't give up on them or the thing God may be after in their story, but I don't always need to hear everything. I am not "holier than thou," but I will not forgo holiness either. Who cares what they think? It is God I report to, and it is my conscience I have to live with.

Using such foresight in our conversations averts future fits of mind, so later we are not plagued with guilt and shame. With these disturbances already moved out of the way, we can spend our energy on praising, worshiping, and adoring God rather than trying to climb out of the muck.

We get to know God through prayer. He changes our hearts and minds through prayer. We come to know His provision and power in prayer. We *ginosko* know God through prayer. We wait on God in prayer.

Everything that goes into a life of pleasing God has been miraculously given to us by getting to know, personally and intimately, the One who invited us to God. The best invitation we ever received! We were also given absolutely terrific promises to pass on to you— your tickets to participation in the life of God after you turned your back on a world corrupted by lust.

So don't lose a minute in building on what you've been given, complementing your basic faith with good character, spiritual understanding, alert discipline, passionate patience, reverent wonder, warm friendliness, and generous love, each dimension fitting into and developing the others. With these qualities active and growing in your lives, no grass will grow under your feet, no day will pass without its reward as you mature in your experience of our Master Jesus. (2 Pet. 1:3–9 MSG)

Prayer matures us in experiencing our Master Jesus. And experiencing Jesus goes about transforming our minds into His likeness, His love, and His mercy.

Journal: God, what are You speaking to me? What are You calling me to? How do I do this?

_____

_____

_____

_____

_____

—————— **Free Download** ——————

Download a printable Power Prayer Sheet with mind-steadying prayers at www.itakethoughtscaptive.com.

Conclusion

What You Need to Know to Carry On

Your worst days are never so bad that you are beyond the *reach* of God's grace. And your best days are never so good that you are beyond the *need* of God's grace.

Jerry Bridges, *The Discipline of Grace*

God is big enough to keep us. God is good enough to lead us. God is strong enough to make us. God is faithful enough to love us. And God is powerful enough to do anything He wants. Nothing can stop the Lord who is almighty. No powers of hell. No sin or death. No plan of humankind. No walls. No hindrances. No blockages. No schemes of the enemy. No mindsets.

Transformed minds walk with the mind of Christ. They know that God's will shall be done. Transformed minds understand God is sovereign over everything. They *ginosko* know that "at the name of Jesus every knee should bow, in heaven and on earth and under the earth" (Phil. 2:10).

The immensity of His majesty overcomes them. It is not a hard-fought battle to overcome lies, because the truth of Jesus—His kingdom, His majesty, His power to deliver and to break strongholds—is far weightier than any lie trying to torment us. Any falsehood is measly compared with the all-surpassing glory of King Jesus and the blood He has shed. "Jesus [is] the mediator of a new covenant, and [we have come] to the sprinkled blood that *speaks a better word* than the blood of Abel" (Heb. 12:24, emphasis added).

For those with the mind of Christ, the blood is speaking a better word, and they know it intimately. When this happens, Jesus is a living reality, working and moving in and through the lover, the yielded vessel, the moldable clay. Jesus fills everything, everywhere, with Himself. "And the church is his body; it is made full and complete by Christ, who fills all things everywhere with himself" (Eph. 1:23 NLT).

The living absoluteness of Jesus surrounds and fills those yielded, surrendered, and connected to the mind of Christ. We know everything is by Him, from Him, and to Him. This is joy. Getting to love and to know Jesus is joy. Someday, every crown gained on earth *from Him* will be thrown down *to Him*. We can be blown away by the idea that it is all from Jesus, about Jesus, and back to Jesus. Glory to God!

A renewed and transformed mind doesn't rely on its own flesh. Self-centered ruminations and self-protection measures are left at the altar in the face of His power, glory, and care. His incomparable beauty is what a hungry and thirsty soul needs. Knowing Him is loving Him. And knowing Him is also finding purpose. For in this place, His purpose calls. And, best of all, He is the One "who works in you to will and to act *in order to fulfill* his good purpose" (Phil. 2:13).

The pressure is off of us, because the cross was carried by Him.

Isn't Jesus astounding? His thoughts are above ours. His ways are not our ways. We must return to this truth often. For we will not always understand what God is purposing; His plans transcend every facet of our natural minds.

"'What no eye has seen, what no ear has heard, and what no human mind has conceived'—the things God has prepared for those who love him" (1 Cor. 2:9). Beyond us is what God has prepared for us. This is why we have to get out of our own minds.

What does it matter if we know everything? Eve sought to know everything. How did that serve her? God knows what He is doing. Isn't that enough? What is trust if it has to know everything? What is faith if it has to see everything? His ways transcend mental understanding. He has good endings for those with humble beginnings. He has a good plan for those who love Him. "Everyone who believes in him will not be put to shame" (Rom. 10:11 ESV).

Why do I say all this? Because we can rest in the work that Jesus has done. We don't strive for the mind of Christ; we receive it by the Spirit of God. Even when we don't know what to pray, "the Spirit Himself intercedes for us with groans too deep for words" (8:26 BSB). We are not going at this alone. We have a Helper, Counselor, and Guide: the Holy Spirit.

"For *in him* we live and move and have our being" (Acts 17:28). The Spirit of Christ is in you, dear one. You are never alone. Christ-in-you does not leave you unprotected (2 Cor. 13:5).

Even more than being safe, though, we receive something far greater. It is this: as we know Him and behold Him, we become more like Him. "And we all, with unveiled face, beholding the glory of the Lord, are being transformed into the same image from one degree of glory to another. For this comes from the Lord who is the Spirit" (3:18 ESV).

Beholding is how we go about holding the character and life of Christ within us that wants to work through us. As we seize this, it changes everything. We wonder rather than worry. We marvel instead of marginalizing ourselves. We exalt Him versus excommunicating people because we are offended by them.

God's incredibility surpasses all the insanity surrounding us. We fall into prayer, worship, and praise more easily. Wrong things we figured about God are shaken off, and a new perspective takes form and shape. We believe God is who He professes to be. We don't just read about Him; we know Him! We don't just know theology; we are a walking testimony of His goodness and grace.

Here we begin to think as Christ thinks. We love as Christ loves. His Word becomes our word. His thoughts drive all we do, see, say, behold, process, think about, and release. His compassion is our embrace. His suffering is our call to love people. His life laid down is our calling to do the same.

This embodies transformation.

You have everything you need, through Christ Jesus, to be transformed. May you stay your mind on Jesus as you fight the good fight of faith with a steady mind and a strong heart. May His thoughts be your thoughts. May His heart consume your heart. And may His hands and feet send you out to accomplish all His will. May you experience His love and "be made complete with all the fullness of life and power that comes from God" (Eph. 3:19 NLT).

And before we go, here are three more verses to cling to as you embark on your journey of walking with Jesus. I hope they bless you as they have me. I have grasped these truths with much hope and in deep need during hard times. I have full faith that they will increase your life as they have mine.

He keeps "in perfect peace [the person] whose mind is stayed on [Him]" (Isa. 26:3 ESV).

"The peace of God . . . will guard your [heart and mind] in Christ Jesus" (Phil. 4:7).

You have not been given "a spirit of fear and timidity, but of power, love, and self-discipline" (2 Tim. 1:7 NLT).

Father, thank You that "I can do all this through him who gives me strength" (Phil. 4:13). Thank You that "in all these things we are more than conquerors through him who loved us" (Rom. 8:37). Thank You that I have the mind of Christ to instruct me. Thank You that all my fountains are in You. Thank You that You are the Prince of Peace. Thank You that I am safe in You. Thank You that You are my hope of all glory, and You live inside me. Thank You that, by the Spirit, I can know "the wonderful things God has freely given us" (1 Cor. 2:12 NLT). Thank You that "no eye has seen, no ear has heard, and no mind has imagined what God has prepared for those who love him" (v. 9 NLT).

Thank You for wanting me. Thank You for choosing me. I am so blessed to be Your child. I am so cared for under Your promises the way I am. I want to glorify You with all my thoughts, words, and deeds. Give me that power. Aid me in my going, growing, and becoming. You know I love You! Increase my desire for You. I want You more than life itself. I thank You for all You taught me in this book. I receive everything You have for me. You are faithful to perform Your Word. In You, God, I trust wholeheartedly. In Jesus's name. Amen.

──── Free Download ────

Find the "I Am" statements of Jesus and "I am" statements you can speak over yourself at www.itakethoughtscaptive.com.

Acknowledgments

To God be all the glory!

And to everyone who helped me, prayed for me, loved on me, let me use their home, gave up their time, worked to make this book amazing, and blessed me in the publishing process—you know who you are, and so does God. I pray He richly rewards you.

And thank you.

Appendix

Tools for Sustaining Victory

We must know our thoughts in order to take them captive. In this appendix are three tools to aid you along your thought journey. Two will help you identify your thoughts. Sometimes we aren't even aware of what we are thinking! The third tool, the Power Prayer Guide, is full of prayers so you can receive heavenly help. The goal is for you to get to where you want to go. I hope these tools assist you as you walk out the process of taking every thought captive.

1. Eighty-Five Lies Worth Addressing

1. God doesn't care about me.
2. God doesn't have good things for me.
3. God doesn't want me.
4. God forgets about me.
5. I don't matter.
6. What I do doesn't matter.

7. What I do matters so much that it makes up who I am.

8. Feelings are the ruler of my life.

9. People control me.

10. Circumstances control me.

11. I hate me.

12. I am ugly, fat, stupid, or ___.

13. The world has the answers or the tools I need.

14. People make me or have my solution.

15. If I love myself more, I'll feel happy.

16. I should just do whatever I want to do, so I'll feel happy.

17. God is angry at me for what I do, and He doesn't forgive.

18. I am not good enough to be forgiven.

19. I am a waste of time.

20. I waste time. I make constant mistakes. I am fatally flawed.

21. I can't be fixed.

22. I am a loser.

23. I am going to be like my dad or mom.

24. Power, prestige, and purpose will make me love myself or be loved.

25. I have to be seen to be valuable.

26. I need to have ___ to feel ___.

27. I have to take power or else ___ will happen.

28. I am a bad parent, and my kids are all my fault.

29. Men or women will always rule over me.

30. I am a burden.

31. I am too ___ to be loved.

32. I have no control over my feelings.

33. There are no trials or tribulations.

34. I am bad if I have feelings.

35. I need different gifts or talents.

36. I need to be better, funnier, smarter, or ___.

37. My voice doesn't matter or isn't accepted.

38. I am nothing special.

39. It's okay to compare myself to other people.

40. It's all about sex. I am a sex symbol or used for sexual means.

41. I am powerful when I have control.

42. I'll never be close to God.

43. I'll never change.

44. I'll never know my real identity.

45. I'll never measure up.

46. I won't make it.

47. I have to do more to be more loved.

48. I have to do everything perfectly.

49. I have to compete to prove my worth.

50. I am only loved when I am serving.

51. I have to be who others want me to be.

52. God's way is not the best way.

53. My brokenness is too much for God.

54. I can't be honest before God, because He may not like me.

55. I can't get anything right.

56. Messed-up people aren't really saved.

57. God only likes me when I am doing good.

58. My race, income level, or appearance limits how God can use me.

59. It's selfish to rest, receive, or take care of me.

60. I am not allowed to be me.

61. I am not allowed to sit down.

62. I am alone, and no one understands.

63. I am not liked by anyone.

64. I don't fit in and never will.

65. God is annoyed at me.

66. God won't be there for me.

67. God doesn't see my needs.

68. I am too late, too old, or too slow to get things.

69. I've wasted too much time, and now my opportunity is gone.

70. I am lost and can't be found again.

71. All the trauma I've gone through can't be healed.

72. There are only so many chances, and all mine are gone.

73. The Word of God is just empty promises.

74. I can't outlive my past.

75. I need to be married, have kids, or look a certain way to be valued.

76. God can't be trusted to protect me.

77. God can't be trusted to help me.

78. God can't help me enough to save me.

79. I am unsavable.

80. I am hopeless.

81. I have to meet the world's standard or I am dirt.

82. I am what is happening to me.

83. I am what has been spoken over me.

84. I can fix myself by beating myself up.

85. I can fix things alone.

2. Daily Thought Tracker

Think about what you are thinking about by tracking your thoughts for a week.

Get a blank sheet of paper. Write down any thought that you sense needs to be taken captive (anything negative, fearful, anxious, from the enemy, prideful, selfish, and so on). Start each day at the top of a fresh page. At the end of the week, review your daily lists and notice any thought themes. This will help you understand more of what is going on in your heart.

Here is an example of how it may look:

Day 1

> *I am fat.*
> *I am not a good mom.*

Themes

3. Power Prayer Guide

Personalize these prayers with your name or your family's name, and with I-statements.

> *May I "be joyful in hope, patient in affliction, faithful in prayer" (Rom. 12:12).*

God, help me to not be "anxious about anything, but in every situation, by prayer and petition, with thanksgiving, present [my] requests to God. And the peace of God, which transcends all understanding, will guard [my heart and mind] in Christ Jesus" (Phil. 4:6–7).

"May the Lord make [my] love increase and overflow for . . . everyone else. . . . . May he strengthen [my heart] so that [I] will be blameless and holy in the presence of [my] God and Father when [my] Lord Jesus comes with all his holy ones" (1 Thess. 3:12–13).

God, fill me "with the knowledge of [your] will through all the wisdom and understanding that the Spirit gives, so that [I] may live a life worthy of the Lord" (Col. 1:9–10).

May "the God of our Lord Jesus Christ, the glorious Father, [give me] the Spirit of wisdom and revelation, so that [I] may know him better. I pray that the eyes of [my] heart may be enlightened in order that [I] may know the hope to which he has called [me], the riches of his glorious inheritance in his holy people, and his incomparably great power for us who believe. That power is the same as the mighty strength he exerted when he raised Christ from the dead and seated him at his right hand in the heavenly realms, far above all rule and authority, power and dominion, and every name that is invoked, not only in the present age but also in the one to come. And God placed all things under his feet and appointed him to be head over everything for the church, which is his body, the fullness of him who fills everything in every way" (Eph. 1:17–23).

"I kneel before the Father, from whom every family in heaven and on earth derives its name. I pray that out of his glorious

riches he may strengthen [me] with power through his Spirit in [my] inner being, so that Christ may dwell in [my heart] through faith. And I pray that [I], being rooted and established in love, may have power, together with all the Lord's holy people, to grasp how wide and long and high and deep is the love of Christ, and to know this love that surpasses knowledge—that [I] may be filled to the measure of all the fullness of God. Now to him who is able to do immeasurably more than all we ask or imagine, according to his power that is at work within us, to him be glory in the church and in Christ Jesus throughout all generations, for ever and ever! Amen" (Eph. 3:14–21).

"Now may the Lord of peace himself give [me] peace at all times and in every way. The Lord be with [me]" (2 Thess. 3:16).

"May the God of hope fill [me] with all joy and peace as [I] trust in him, so that [I] may overflow with hope by the power of the Holy Spirit" (Rom. 15:13).

For more tools and resources to help you along your way, visit www.itake thoughtscaptive.com.

Notes

Chapter 2 Be a Warrior!

1. Alex Dopico, "Did the Romans Take Prisoners of War?," Janet-Panic World History Portal, December 22, 2020, https://janetpanic.com/did-the-romans-take -prisoners-of-war.

Chapter 3 Believe You're Worthy of a Changed Mind

1. "The Story of How God Called Billy Graham," Billy Graham Evangelistic Association UK, accessed July 12, 2022, https://billygraham.org.uk/billy-grahams -story.

Chapter 5 Allow Experience to Transcend Knowledge

1. Kendra Cherry, "What Is Neuroplasticity?," Very Well Mind, February 18, 2022, https://www.verywellmind.com/what-is-brain-plasticity-2794886.

2. The KJV New Testament Greek Lexicon, s.v. "ginosko," Bible Study Tools, accessed July 13, 2022, https://www.biblestudytools.com/lexicons/greek/kjv/ ginosko.html.

Chapter 6 Respond, Don't React

1. Sara Smart, "Maryland Homeowners Burned Down Their Home While Attempting to Rid the House of Snakes," CNN, December 3, 2021, https://www .cnn.com/2021/12/03/us/house-fire-snake-removal-trnd/index.html.

2. Merriam-Webster Dictionary, s.v. "understanding," accessed July 14, 2022, https://www.merriam-webster.com/dictionary/understanding.

3. "Strong's G1271: *Dianoia*," Blue Letter Bible, accessed August 29, 2022, https://www.blueletterbible.org/lexicon/g1271/kjv/tr/0-1.

Chapter 7 Say, "Shut Up, Devil!"

1. "Strong's G2706: *kataphroneō*," Blue Letter Bible, accessed August 29, 2022, https://www.blueletterbible.org/lexicon/g2706/kjv/tr/0-1.

Chapter 8 Avoid This Mentality at All Costs

1. Merriam-Webster Dictionary, s.v. "corrupt," accessed July 18, 2022, https://www.merriam-webster.com/dictionary/corrupt.

2. Dennis Prager, *Happiness Is a Serious Problem: A Human Nature Repair Manual* (New York: ReganBooks, 1998), 59, emphasis in original.

Chapter 9 Adopt These Eight Heart Postures

1. Dale Carnegie, *How to Win Friends and Influence People* (New York: Pocket Books, 1936), 20.

Chapter 11 Break Down the Lie of "I Am Not Enough or Don't Have Enough"

1. Alex Daniel, "20 Crazy Valuable Things You Probably Owned and Threw Out," BestLife, November 27, 2018, https://bestlifeonline.com/crazy-valuable-tossed-items.

Chapter 16 An Overcomer's Guide to Keeping Thoughts Captive

1. This idea is influenced by a quote from Lysa TerKeurst, "A disappointment can sometimes be a divine appointment in disguise." Proverbs 31 (@Proverbs 31org), "A disappointment can sometimes," Twitter, November 12, 2015, https://twitter.com/Proverbs31org/status/664960149329580037.

Kelly Balarie is the author of *Fear Fighting, Battle Ready,* and *Rest Now.* When speaking at women's conferences around the nation, Kelly delights in joining hands with women as they go through life's ups and downs. To see marriages restored, hope recovered, and prayers of faith lifted up to a God on the move are some of her greatest joys. Beyond this, Kelly has led spiritual growth Bible study groups and has been seen on *TODAY, The 700 Club,* Cross walk.com, iBelieve.com, and (in)courage. Her work has also been featured by *Relevant* and *Today's Christian Woman.* She lives with her husband and two kiddos on the East Coast.

YOU CAN LIVE
VICTORIOUSLY.

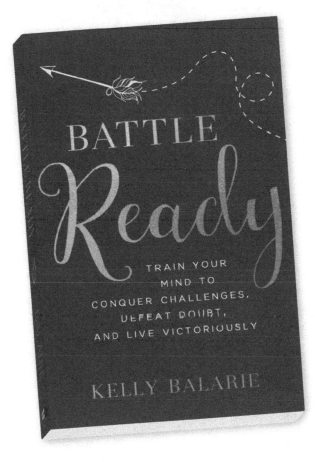

Battle Ready is a hands-on scriptural plan
that teaches you twelve easy-to-implement,
confidence-building mindsets designed to
transform your thoughts and, therefore, your life.

Your Permission to
Breathe and Grow

Rest Now helps you create healthy boundaries
as you stop striving for rest and start
living *from* it—like Jesus did.

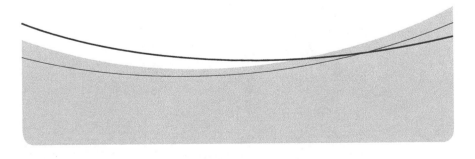